Inquiry-Based Learning

Arts, Creativities, and Learning Environments in Global Perspectives

Series Editors

Tatiana Chemi (*Aalborg University*)
Anu M. Mitra (*Union Institute & University*)
Chunfang Zhou (*Aalborg University*)

VOLUME 4

The titles published in this series are listed at *brill.com/acle*

Inquiry-Based Learning

A Guidebook to Writing a Science Opera

By

Irma Smegen and Oded Ben-Horin

BRILL
SENSE

LEIDEN | BOSTON

Cover illustration: Scene from *Skylight*, photograph by Curso de Música Silva Monteiro, Porto, Portugal

All chapters in this book have undergone peer review.

Library of Congress Cataloging-in-Publication Data

Names: Smegen, Irma, author. | Ben-Horin, Oded, author.
Title: Inquiry-based learning : a guidebook to writing a science opera / By
  Irma Smegen and Oded Ben-Horin.
Description: Leiden ; Boston : Brill | Sense, [2021] | Series: Arts,
  creativities, and learning environments in global perspectives,
  2589-9813 ; Volume 4 | Includes bibliographical references.
Identifiers: LCCN 2020037963 (print) | LCCN 2020037964 (ebook) | ISBN
  9789004436497 (paperback) | ISBN 9789004436503 (hardback) | ISBN
  9789004436510 (ebook)
Subjects: LCSH: Inquiry-based learning. | Science--Study and teaching. |
  Opera--Study and teaching.
Classification: LCC LB1027.23 .S58 2021 (print) | LCC LB1027.23 (ebook) |
  DDC 371.39--dc23
LC record available at https://lccn.loc.gov/2020037963
LC ebook record available at https://lccn.loc.gov/2020037964

Typeface for the Latin, Greek, and Cyrillic scripts: "Brill". See and download: brill.com/brill-typeface.

ISSN 2589-9813
ISBN 978-90-04-43649-7 (paperback)
ISBN 978-90-04-43650-3 (hardback)
ISBN 978-90-04-43651-0 (e-book)

Copyright 2021 by Koninklijke Brill NV, Leiden, The Netherlands.
Koninklijke Brill NV incorporates the imprints Brill, Brill Hes & De Graaf, Brill Nijhoff, Brill Rodopi, Brill Sense, Hotei Publishing, mentis Verlag, Verlag Ferdinand Schöningh and Wilhelm Fink Verlag.
All rights reserved. No part of this publication may be reproduced, translated, stored in a retrieval system, or transmitted in any form or by any means, electronic, mechanical, photocopying, recording or otherwise, without prior written permission from the publisher. Requests for re-use and/or translations must be addressed to Koninklijke Brill NV via brill.com or copyright.com.

This book is printed on acid-free paper and produced in a sustainable manner.

To Coen and Anna
– Irma Smegen

•••

To Rebekka Kirsten
– Oded Ben-Horin

Contents

Foreword   IX
   Carl Pennypacker
Acknowledgements   XII
List of Figures and Tables   XIV
About the Authors   XVII

Introduction: For the Teachers   1

PART 1
Ideas for Inquiry

1 **Inquiry-Based Learning with Write a Science Opera**   5
   1   What Is Inquiry-Based Learning?   6
   2   Why Is This Important?   6
   3   What Attitude Will You Need as a WASO Teacher?   7
   4   Why Use Opera?   8

2 **Write a Science Opera (WASO)**   10
   1   What Is Opera?   10
   2   What Is Write a Science Opera?   10
   3   The History   11
   4   Research Results   13
   5   How Much Time Does It Take?   14
   6   Can All Children Join?   14
   7   Examples of Write a Science Opera Projects   15
   8   WASO Going Viral: Global Science Opera   16

3 **Relations to Multiple School Subjects in the Curriculum**   21
   1   Teaching School Subjects through WASO   22
   2   Teaching Creativity and Entrepreneurship through WASO   25
   3   Teaching Sustainability through WASO   28

PART 2
Let's Go!

4 **Warming Up**   33
   1   Body   34

    2   Voice   36
    3   Body and Voice   36
    4   Acting Exercises   37
    5   Concentration Exercises   40
    6   Cooperative Exercises   42

5 **Write a Science Opera in Thirteen to Fifteen Steps**   45

6 **Write a Science Opera in Seven to Eleven Steps**   64

7 **Assigning the Tasks**   70
    1   Directing   71
    2   Assistant Directing   74
    3   The Libretto   74
    4   Acting   77
    5   Music   78
    6   Set Designing   81
    7   Props   82
    8   Costumes   83
    9   Make-Up   84
    10 Dance   85
    11 Technology   86
    12 Public Relations   88
    13 Project Management   88

8 **Extras to Think of When Performing**   90
    1   Safety   90
    2   Preparations   91
    3   Stress Less   91
    4   Making Mistakes   93
    5   Asking Questions   94

9 **Evaluation**   95
    1   Frequency   96
    2   Objective of the Evaluation   96
    3   Other Ways of Evaluating   96
    4   Final Evaluation   98

Appendix 1: Ways of Making Groups   101
Appendix 2: Role Descriptions   104
Appendix 3: Strategic Partnership: Agents of Change (space) – Pedagogical Framework   106

Foreword

Carl Pennypacker

It has been my distinct honour and pleasure to witness multiple groups and school classes writing science operas. The enthusiasm, the level of creativity, the model building, and the performances of these operas have been beautiful and helped inform students, teachers, and my scientific view of the world. I am convinced that science opera writing will find a larger and larger home amongst science and arts educators, and indeed be a place where the modern issues of science and art can be played out on a grand stage, with the splendour and ceremony of a grand opera.

And indeed, society itself faces many existential crises, including climate change, over-population, fair distribution and sharing of resources. Such issues deserve the stage and the splendour of opera. Science operas can give voice to these concerns.

One of the factors in science operas' favour, is that I find that enabling students to frame and perform their learning helps them learn better than they do with traditional methods, and starts their minds on a personal and collective journey engaged in ways to improve the world.

Since its invention 400 years ago, opera has metamorphosed through several stages, with evolution of characters and stories found in Greek drama to the classical period, where characters and plots were increasingly related to real life. This change must almost certainly be related to the other changes in civilisation.

Now, I feel that a new stage of opera is justified, based on humanity's much clearer, more detailed, and explicit understanding of science and the universe. Science and technology have revolutionised all of human life and endeavours, so it is really appropriate to further humanise opera with tales, stories, and explications of scientific endeavour that reach across scientific disciplines, characters, periods, and themes. All are logical plot and source material for science operas.

One might wonder why science operas have not been performed or attempted as a system before now. Thinking about the global developments which build upon the science operas described in this book, one speculation would be that, in fact, *The Two Cultures* as C.P. Snow described them, are an artefact of pre-Global Science Opera society.[1] In Snow's own words: "So the great edifice of modern physics goes up, and the majority of the cleverest people in the western world have about as much insight into it as their Neolithic ancestors would have had" (1998, pp. 14–15). Science operas are a sturdy and strong bridge between Snow's cultures.

The people of the world must learn more science and math if we are to prevent the earth from dying. This is a huge problem in the United States. As of this writing, some world leaders are able to ignore the overwhelming body of evidence that humans are causing climate change. And this ignorance might lead to the death of our planet. It is also easily proven that most Americans need to get better at simple math. Work by Eric Gaze indicates that more than 80% of Americans are illiterate in pre-algebra (proportions, ratios, linear equations), thereby limiting their ability to read graphs, or understand data.

The science writer Timothy Ferris (2010) has traced the development of democracy as due to the proliferation of science and scientific methods. "The democratic revolution was sparked – caused is perhaps not too strong a word – by the scientific revolution, and that science continues to empower political freedom today" (p. 2).

Similarly, science now has the depth and profound understanding of so many important parts of the universe and the earth, perhaps it can begin to unleash a revolution in operas – operas that model, explain, celebrate, hold in wonder, and generally share the heroic view of the universe that we now possess.

As I am a part-science educator, we know from cognitive science that students making models of scientific phenomena is one of the most effective teaching strategies known. Hence, students making models, in the form of creating a science opera, is almost certainly an effective mode of science teaching. Science is often felt to be beautiful and heroic by scientists – we scientists need to be engaged in a process where science can become heroic and beautiful for all people, and science operas are a great way to do this!

So, in conclusion, it is time for opera to catch up with our modern world, and allow the proliferation of powerful science and education through the composition, staging, and performance of science operas. Global Science Operas are true pathfinders for the world at large, and I feel privileged to play a modest supporting role in the chorus.

Note

1   Global Science Opera, www.globalscienceopera.com

References

Ferris, T. (2010). *The science of liberty: Democracy, reason, and the laws of nature.* New York, NY: Harper Collins.

Snow, C. P. (1998). *The two cultures.* Cambridge, UK: Cambridge University Press.

Acknowledgements

We wish to thank the persons, institutions, initiatives, and projects which have contributed to this book. Many of these have been directly associated with the authoring of the book and with the European Commission's Erasmus+ project Strategic Partnership: Agents of Change in Education (SPACE) which provided the framework for the book's development.[1] These include the SPACE project partner institutions Artesis Plantijn University College in Belgium; the European Network for Opera and Dance Education (RESEO) in Belgium; Dundalk Institute of Technology in Ireland; Speel je Wijs in the Netherlands; Western Norway University of Applied Science in Norway; and Curso de Música Silva Monteiro in Portugal. We would also like to thank the following institutions, initiatives, and projects who contributed to the development of WASO before and during the SPACE project's existence in a large variety of ways. Of these, the most profound contribution was made by the European projects which, through their publication and sharing of open-access WASO materials, provided examples and materials, and invited us, as authors, to build upon their experiences and findings. For this, we are truly grateful:
- Implementing Creative Strategies into Science Teaching (CREAT-IT): European Commission 2013–2015.[2]
- Write a Science Opera (WASO): European Economic Area 2014–2016.
- Developing an Engaging Science Classroom (CREATIONS): European Commission 2015–2018.[3]
- Compenta: Cultuureducatie met Kwaliteit in the Netherlands 2017.

We would also like to thank the following for their contributions to WASO during the past years: the University and College Network for Western Norway (UH-nett Vest, Norway), University of Bergen (Norway), University of Stavanger (Norway), the Stord/Haugesund University College K-PED programme and CASE centre (Norway), the Bergen National Opera (Norway), Science View (Greece), Ellinogermaniki Agogi (Greece), the Royal Opera House Education Department (UK), Galileo Teacher Training Programme (Portugal), Global Hands on Universe (USA), the European Space Agency's European Space Technology and Research Centre (ESTEC, the Netherlands).

We thank all the schools, universities, kindergartens, science institutions, and opera and art institutions which invited the different WASO teams into their premises since the year 2011 to implement, evaluate, analyse, enjoy, risk, learn, discuss, critique, and further develop the WASO experience together with us.

We thank Marieke McBean and Magne Espeland for their valuable comments during the final stages of writing this book.

ACKNOWLEDGEMENTS

Finally, the authors wish to thank the Global Science Opera participants for allowing WASO to be implemented on a global stage.

Notes

1. Project website: www.steameducation.eu
2. See www.creatit-project.eu
3. See www.creations-project.eu

Figures and Tables

Figures

1. Enjoy WASO. Photograph: Curso de Música Silva Monteiro Porto, Portugal, http://cmsilvamonteiro.com/   2
2. Could you please explain? Photograph: Joanne Bartol, the Netherlands.   4
3. Inquiry-based learning. Photograph: Curso de Música Silva Monteiro Porto, Portugal, http://cmsilvamonteiro.com/   5
4. In Write a Science Opera both the process and the product are equally important. Photograph: Petra Moedt, Emmaschool Steenwijk, the Netherlands.   7
5. Opera. Photograph: Curso de Música Silva Monteiro Porto, Portugal, http://cmsilvamonteiro.com/   8
6. Write a Science Opera. Photograph: Curso de Música Silva Monteiro Porto, Portugal, http://cmsilvamonteiro.com/   11
7. WASO project in Uganda. Photograph: Jimmy Olega, Steiner School, Arua, Uganda.   12
8. *Skylight*. Photograph: Henk de Reus, de Reus Projects, the Netherlands, www.dereusprojects.com   16
9. Earth. Photograph: Curso de Música Silva Monteiro Porto, Portugal, http://cmsilvamonteiro.com/   17
10. *Moon Village*. Image credit: European Space Agency. Poster by the Global Science Opera. Design: Janne Robberstad, www.globalscienceopera.com   19
11. Connecting with other subjects. Photograph: Curso de Música Silva Monteiro Porto, Portugal, http://cmsilvamonteiro.com/   22
12. Expression. Photograph: Rianne Hofma, Vensterschool, Noordwolde, the Netherlands.   23
13. Let's dance.   25
14. Sewing. Photograph: Curso de Música Silva Monteiro Porto, Portugal, http://cmsilvamonteiro.com/   26
15. Let's go! Photograph: Rianne Hofma, Vensterschool, Noordwolde, the Netherlands.   32
16. Warming up. Photograph: Curso de Música Silva Monteiro Porto, Portugal, http://cmsilvamonteiro.com/   33
17. Watching in the mirror. Photograph: Curso de Música Silva Monteiro Porto, Portugal, http://cmsilvamonteiro.com/   35
18. Greeting. Photograph: Petra Moedt, Emmaschool Steenwijk, the Netherlands.   38
19. Names.   40

FIGURES AND TABLES   XV

20 Hand on blue. Photograph: Ilse Kruid, OBS Op 't Veld, Emmen, the Netherlands.   42
21 Two noses. Photograph: Petra Moedt, Emmaschool Steenwijk, the Netherlands.   43
22 Let's WASO! Photograph: Curso de Música Silva Monteiro Porto, Portugal, http://cmsilvamonteiro.com/   45
23 Mind map.   51
24 Thinking of questions. Photograph: Curso de Música Silva Monteiro Porto, Portugal, http://cmsilvamonteiro.com/   51
25 More scientific research might be needed. Photograph: Curso de Música Silva Monteiro Porto, Portugal, http://cmsilvamonteiro.com/   52
26 Tableau vivant. Photograph: Kristin Saltkjelvik, Norway.   54
27 Silhouette. Photograph: Rianne Hofma, Vensterschool, Noordwolde, the Netherlands.   57
28 Perform. Photograph: Marieke McBean Photography, UK, http://www.marieke.co.uk   62
29 Let's WASO again! Photograph: Marieke McBean Photography, UK, https://marieke.co.uk   64
30 The power of puppets. Photograph: Martine Goulmy, Alles Cats, the Netherlands, www.allescats.com   66
31 Dancing. Photograph: Petra Moedt, Emmaschool Steenwijk, the Netherlands.   67
32 The performance. Photograph: Petra Moedt, Emmaschool Steenwijk, the Netherlands.   69
33 Different tasks. Photograph: Joanne Bartol, the Netherlands.   70
34 Run-through. Photograph: Curso de Música Silva Monteiro Porto, Portugal, http://cmsilvamonteiro.com/   73
35 Working on the script. Photograph: Marieke McBean Photography, UK, http://www.marieke.co.uk   75
36 Use the talents in your group. Photograph: Yaron Ben-Horin, Israel.   76
37 Passengers duet. Photograph: Curso de Música Silva Monteiro Porto, Portugal, http://cmsilvamonteiro.com/   81
38 Less is more.   82
39 Well-chosen costumes. Photograph: Nirith Ben-Horin, Israel.   83
40 Princess doing her make-up. Photograph: Marieke McBean Photography, UK, http://www.marieke.co.uk   84
41 Let's dance again! Photograph: Curso de Música Silva Monteiro Porto, Portugal, http://cmsilvamonteiro.com/   85
42 Shadow play. Photograph: Curso de Música Silva Monteiro Porto, Portugal, http://cmsilvamonteiro.com/   86

43   Mysterious light. Photograph: Curso de Música Silva Monteiro Porto, Portugal, http://cmsilvamonteiro.com/   87
44   Don't forget the flowers. Photograph: Curso de Música Silva Monteiro Porto, Portugal, http://cmsilvamonteiro.com/   89
45   Think of ... Photograph: Curso de Música Silva Monteiro Porto, Portugal, http://cmsilvamonteiro.com/   90
46   You are beautiful. Photograph: Curso de Música Silva Monteiro Porto, Portugal, http://cmsilvamonteiro.com/   92
47   Don't ever be afraid to ask a question. Photograph: Curso de Música Silva Monteiro Porto, Portugal, http://cmsilvamonteiro.com/   94
48   Helping each other grow. Photograph: Curso de Música Silva Monteiro Porto, Portugal, http://cmsilvamonteiro.com/   95
49   Add happiness to your world each day. Photograph: Rianne Hofma, Vensterschool, Noordwolde, the Netherlands.   99
50   Image of a huge, handle-shaped prominence taken on September 14, 1999. Prominences are huge clouds of relatively cool dense plasma suspended in the Sun's hot, thin corona. At times, they can erupt, escaping the Sun's atmosphere. Photo credit: SOHO [ESA and NASA].   114

Tables

1   WASO in thirteen to fifteen steps.   46
2   Examples of scientific subjects.   47
3   Distributing the tasks.   59
4   Example of an alternative script design.   76

About the Authors

Irma Smegen

(1970) lives in the Netherlands and is a drama teacher, kindergarten and elementary school teacher. After having worked 18 years as a professor of drama, arts and culture at the teacher education program of Stenden University, Irma is now spending all her time working for her own company Speel je Wijs.

With Speel je Wijs (Play to wisdom/Play your own tune), Irma is internationally known for her work in promoting arts, STEAM, and mindfulness in education. She writes educational books, develops learning materials, gives lectures, and provides training courses to inspire professionals working with children. Playing and playful learning are always the main ingredients in her work.

More information: www.irmasmegen.com

Oded Ben-Horin

(1970) is Head of Department of Arts Education at Western Norway University of Applied Sciences. Oded coordinates the Global Science Opera, and is a co-developer of that concept. He is the main developer of the Write a Science Opera (WASO) educational approach to interdisciplinary science/art integration in schools. Oded has led WASO workshops at the Norwegian Opera (Oslo), the Flemish Opera (Antwerp) and the Louis Cruls Astronomy Club (Campos,

Brazil) among others. He has led several European initiatives in the field of creativity in education. Oded is a jazz musician and an Associate Professor of music.

More information: www.hvl.no/ik, www.casecenter.no, www.globalscienceopera.com

• • •

In 2008, Oded and Irma met in Antwerp, Belgium, where they both led workshops at the International Week of Art Education at AP University College. Since then, they became friends and have cooperated in several educational projects.

INTRODUCTION

For the Teachers

Write a Science Opera (WASO) is a transdisciplinary, inquiry-based approach to teaching at the intersection of art and science in schools. In this guidebook, we provide a step-by-step description of how teachers may implement WASO with their pupils.

Implementing WASO is challenging, but the rewards are endless, robust and powerful. It is always surprising regardless of the age of your pupils, the language they speak, or the scientific themes you choose to work with.

This book is not a science education book. Nor is it an arts education book. It is, in many ways, both of these. Yet we aim for it to be something beyond that. While we have provided many details describing how WASO may be implemented, we do not claim to know what the *best* way to do that is. Rather, we invite you to use this book as a doorway to a journey at the intersection of science and the arts. A journey defined by your pupils' curiosity, personal interests and motivations. Indeed, it is the fact that your pupils will be taking charge of their own learning which emboldens us to describe that learning as inquiry-based. And it is the fact that they will be negotiating that learning in both the arts and science which enables us to describe it as transdisciplinary.

WASO thus aims for something specific which, we are sure, you will be able to achieve. Yet you must be willing to dare. You must be willing to leave behind some practices and procedures with which you currently feel very comfortable, even if only for a short time. WASO is a process of constantly choosing from amongst many different possibilities and never looking back. Similarly, we, the authors, have made many choices of what will, and will not, be included in this book. WASO's "specialty" is its combining elements from different disciplines into a unique blend. Providing enough detail regarding that path necessitated leaving many other things outside of this book's pages. During this book we sometimes touch upon fields of knowledge and historical traditions which have filled the pages of many other books. We urge you to view our mentioning of these as invitations to explore them beyond the framework of this one. Perhaps even more importantly, WASO is an invitation for you to cooperate with other teachers in your school, and especially those who teach other disciplines than the ones you teach. In this way, available local practices will be drawn upon and integrated into the project, allowing for your own versions of what the transdisciplinary framework can mean and of how inquiry manifests itself in your pupils' creative process.

In this book, we have provided images taken during WASO, or meant to inspire it further. Most of these images relate to arts practices in WASO. WASO's transdisciplinary character does not "favour" any discipline, however. All disciplines are equally important. Indeed, we invite you to look carefully at the provided images and find or imagine the abundance of scientific questions which inspired them.

The book's first three chapters contain information about what WASO is, and how it relates to various school disciplines and subjects. In Chapter 4 you will find physical and vocal warm-ups. Chapters 5 and 6 contain the actual steps which the pupils will carry out during WASO. In Chapter 7 you will find inspiration for assigning pupils the different tasks which they will need to fulfill. In Chapter 8 you will find further suggestions for how to create a performance. Chapter 9 describes possible approaches to WASO's evaluation process. Appendix 1 contains playful ideas for how the division into groups necessary for group work in WASO may be done. Appendix 2 describes how the science opera's characters are developed. Appendix 3 is the pedagogical framework of the European Commission's Erasmus+ project "SPACE". This framework offers a theoretical perspective of what it is about WASO that enables creativity to emerge in the inquiry process.

We are truly delighted that you are joining us, and look forward to hearing about your experiences so that we can learn from you, as you have hopefully learned from us.

Enjoy WASO!

FIGURE 1   Enjoy WASO
PHOTOGRAPH: CURSO DE MÚSICA SILVA MONTEIRO PORTO, PORTUGAL, http://cmsilvamonteiro.com/

PART 1

Ideas for Inquiry

∴

FIGURE 2 Could you please explain?
PHOTOGRAPH: JOANNE BARTOL, THE NETHERLANDS

CHAPTER 1

Inquiry-Based Learning with Write a Science Opera

Children are curious by nature and like to investigate the world around them. Curious children are willing to learn: they want to find solutions, reasons, or answers. They will ask questions and pursue potential discoveries. Creating a science opera will spark their curiosity and encourage them to investigate both art and science.

The aim of Inquiry-Based Learning is both the discovery and generation of knowledge and the formation of good habits of learning. It may support children's development of a large variety of competences related to the way professional researchers work (van Graft & Kemmers, 2006).

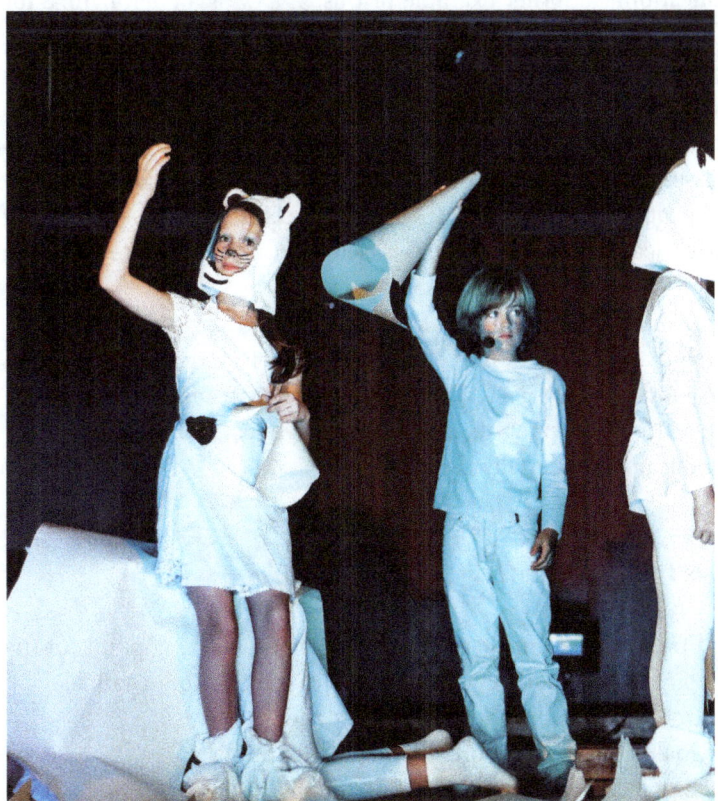

FIGURE 3   Inquiry-based learning
PHOTOGRAPH: CURSO DE MÚSICA SILVA MONTEIRO PORTO, PORTUGAL,
http://cmsilvamonteiro.com/

1 What Is Inquiry-Based Learning?

There are many ways to conceptualise Inquiry-Based Learning (IBL). At the core of them all lies a basic foundation of pupils' curiosity, and the notion that it is that curiosity which drives the pupil's learning. Our claim for a transdisciplinary IBL lies in the fact that we are aiming for an inquiry-based process in both science and the arts. The specific details of what we imply are put forth in the pages below.

1.1 *STEAM Education: An Example of Inquiry-Based Learning*

In ancient Greece, technology and art were closely connected. Today, we are continuously developing our understanding of what such connections may mean for us. The Maker's Movement,[1] in which art and technology lead to new designs, is an example of this quick development.

STEAM education is another example of this. STEAM is an acronym: S for Science, T for Technology, E for Engineering, A for Arts and M for Mathematics. An educational space which brings together science and art subjects. The STEM-subjects have been a recognised combination for some time. In 2006, secondary school teacher Georgette Yakman decided to add the A (for Arts) to her STEM-classes. This proved to be very successful; students were more motivated and often achieved higher grades. Ever since, STEAM has been gaining ground in the educational sector. Inquiry-Based Learning with Write a Science Opera is an example of STEAM education.

Today, several initiatives implement STEAM education as a way to encourage entrepreneurship and innovation in education. One of these is the European Commission's ERASMUS+ project, "Strategic Partnerships: Agents of Change in Education (SPACE)" (see Appendix 3). The SPACE project is the main context within which this book materialised.

2 Why Is This Important?

In each WASO project, a scientific theme is chosen as a starting point for the opera. This choice can be motivated by a variety of reasons, for instance:
- as a first introduction to the chosen scientific theme;
- as a way to make that theme more memorable for pupils;
- as a way of enhancing more traditional ways of teaching.

We understand the creation of an opera as a form of inquiry in which designing happens in many ways. Pupils research the subject of the performance, their roles, the storyline, the emotions as expressed between opera characters, the songs and music, why the story turns out the way it does, how the libretto may best be presented, how music can enhance this, etc. Children often enjoy creating these performances. They collaborate, need each other, investigate their qualities and those of others, further develop these, utilise each other's knowledge and skills, and create a complete opera production together. In addition, an opera brings together several artistic disciplines (visual arts, music, drama, dance and often others), something which provides ample space in which children's creativity may unfold.

Chapter 3 describes how to connect different disciplines, subjects and development areas.

FIGURE 4   In Write a Science Opera both the process and the product are equally important
PHOTOGRAPH: PETRA MOEDT, EMMASCHOOL STEENWIJK, THE NETHERLANDS

3   What Attitude Will You Need as a WASO Teacher?

An important characteristic of Write a Science Opera is its transdisciplinary approach. This implies that you are not only including different disciplines in a single educational setting, but that you are inviting your pupils to understand disciplines in terms of other disciplines. This is an active, creative, and playful way of learning that provides the children with many options. As a teacher, you will not always know beforehand what the process will lead to and how it will proceed.

Teachers who are used to a more pre-determined approach might feel uncertain, but being open to experimenting with the learning process is essential. You may at times be giving less guidance and doing more observation, trusting the children with leading their own learning process.

With this method, children are actively involved and are given freedom of choice, and that is why they will often be more motivated (and sometimes even memorise what they are learning in a completely new way). Knowledge is not transferred to the children; they need to find it themselves in order to proceed with creating their opera. It is the teacher's job to motivate and encourage, to ask questions, and to teach the children to ask questions.

4 Why Use Opera?

In opera, interaction between the various arts disciplines (music, drama, visual arts, and others) creates an exciting space for creative activity.

We would like to acknowledge, however, the importance of other arts and arts education genres such as theatre and musicals. Opera does differ from these in distinct ways: while theatre may sometimes include music, most theatre does not. Furthermore, while musicals share some of what characterises opera, in opera, librettos are sung: dialogue between characters often relies on recitative whereas spoken dialogue is often the norm in musicals.

However, the lines between these differences are often blurred in WASO. Including some spoken phrases in a WASO performance is certainly acceptable. It is the pupils' inquiry and its results (rather than strictly pre-defined rules) which are the main factors in each WASO implementation's performative outcome.

FIGURE 5 Opera
         PHOTOGRAPH: CURSO DE MÚSICA SILVA MONTEIRO PORTO, PORTUGAL, http://cmsilvamonteiro.com/

Note

1 For an interesting example, see www.makezine.com

Reference

van Graft, M., & Kemmers, P. (2006). *Onderzoekend en ontwerpend leren bij natuur en techniek: Basisdocument over de didactiek voor onderzoekend en ontwerpend leren in het primair onderwijs.* The Hague, the Netherlands: Stichting Platform Bètatechniek.

CHAPTER 2

Write a Science Opera (WASO)

1 What Is Opera?

An opera is a dramatic work in which actors sing their parts. It combines music, drama and the visual arts. The music is often played by an orchestra which is made up of a range of classical instruments. The orchestra is typically, but not always, led by a conductor. On stage, the singers bring the story to life by acting and singing the opera's libretto. Designers, scenographers, choreographers and stage directors work together to create an onstage world for the singers to perform in.

Opera has flourished as a main element in the classical music tradition. The thematic subjects of opera have spanned a wide range over the past centuries. They have included comedy, violence, murder, love, politics, societal class differences and much more. Opera composers have often included whole communities in their stories, sung by a chorus of singers.

Opera has broadened throughout the twentieth and twenty-first centuries to embrace contemporary stories and new forms of music. Likewise, it is now created and performed in many new, different ways. Opera is performed in big opera houses such as La Scala in Milan or the Royal Opera House in London, but also in small theatres, fringe venues, at festivals, on TV, and in the cinema. Opera is also created and performed in town centres, on railway station platforms, in gardens, in local libraries and community centres, and in classrooms and school halls.

Write a Science Opera is concerned with *school* operas: children will write and perform their own science operas as a result of their own creative processes.

2 What Is Write a Science Opera?

Write a Science Opera (WASO) is a transdisciplinary, inquiry-based approach to teaching at the intersection of art and science in schools (Ben-Horin et al., 2017).

In WASO, pupils must understand abstract ideas and principles across disciplinary boundaries, such as:
- What style of music do they think best fits an opera about the solar system?

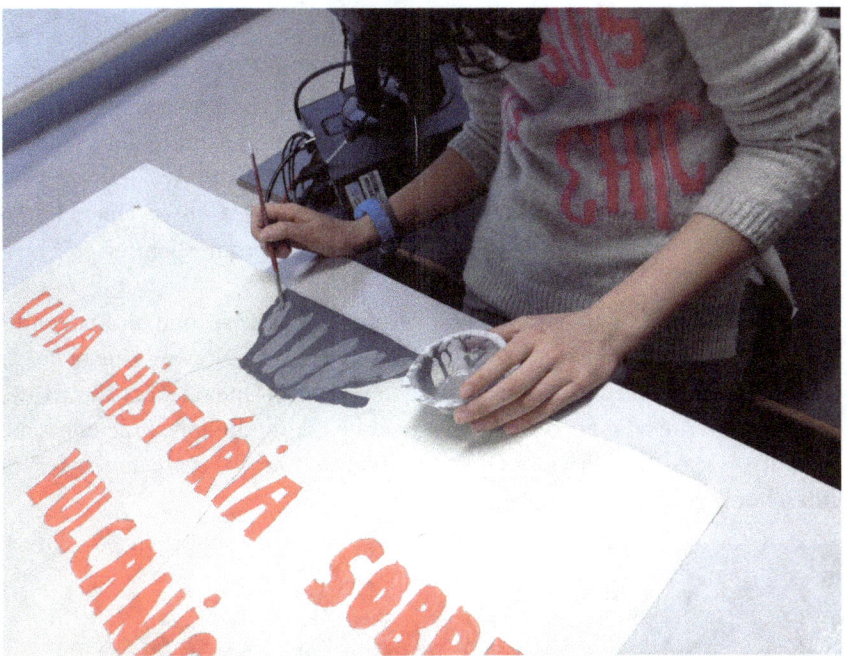

FIGURE 6   Write a Science Opera
PHOTOGRAPH: CURSO DE MÚSICA SILVA MONTEIRO PORTO, PORTUGAL, http://cmsilvamonteiro.com/

– What kind of dramatic dialogue should emerge between characters representing electrons and protons?
– How does the creation of a painting of the ocean impact our questions about the ocean?

These questions are typical of the kind of challenges which arise in WASO. WASO is thus an approach to teaching in which children are invited to take responsibility for their own inquiry, and for the creation of the educational content being explored. WASO is a way of granting children ownership over their learning process.

This guidebook describes the different steps implemented in WASO, including possible variations. The following chapter provides further information on how to Write a Science Opera with pupils.

3   The History

Write an Opera is a creative education method in which opera trainers lead school pupils' creation and performance of original school opera. Originally developed at New York's Metropolitan Opera House, Write an Opera has now been active in Europe for several decades. The Royal Opera House's Education Department in London is credited for implementing the Write an Opera approach in Europe.[1] In Norway, one of the leading locations for Write an Opera training courses is the Western Norway University of Applied Sciences. Several of the arts educators in that institution studied Write an Opera in the Royal Opera House training sessions, and thereafter began themselves teaching others.

Write a Science Opera (WASO) was developed by the second author of this book, Oded Ben-Horin. He began working at Western Norway University of Applied Sciences in 2009. Upon meeting the Write an Opera team at Stord, the concept of Write a Science Opera emerged by asking the following question: What if we used the Write an Opera method to bridge the arts and sciences into school classrooms?

FIGURE 7   WASO project in Uganda
            PHOTOGRAPH: JIMMY OLEGA, STEINER SCHOOL, ARUA, UGANDA

With this question in mind, Ben-Horin and Professor Magne Espeland approached the Royal Opera House's Department of Education and the European Network for Opera and Dance Education (RESEO) to gauge their opinions about this new idea. Both institutions were positive. The effort to try a Write a Science Opera project in a Norwegian school was thus set in motion.

The opportunity to first pilot WASO came about through Bergen National Opera's contact with a Norwegian primary school. For approximately twelve days over the course of several weeks in 2011, biology Professor Karin Pittman, Ben-Horin, and a group of opera artists worked with the sixth graders in order to trial-and-error the creation of a science opera. It was during this project that the team agreed upon two points. First, we were on to something exciting. Second, there was room for much improvement in what we were doing.

During the second WASO implementation with Norwegian ninth graders, the same group of institutions teamed up to implement WASO. This time we were much better prepared to tackle elementary questions which had risen during the first attempt: What is the place of science in an opera? What do we do if the pupils write a science-fiction libretto? How do we evaluate the success (or failure) of the project?

Since that time, dozens of WASO projects have been implemented in approximately forty countries. We have had everything from half-day events to operas that were developed during the course of a full school year. Research, both qualitative and quantitative, has been conducted. WASO has featured in the Norwegian media and, through the Global Science Opera (see below), also in media in Japan, Brazil, the Netherlands, Lithuania, and other countries. WASO projects have produced science operas inspired by a variety of scientific subjects, for example:
– the human body (WASO in Portugal)
– the chemistry of diamonds (WASO in Belgium)
– the northern lights (WASO in Norway)
– the sense of vision (WASO in Scotland)
– supernovae (WASO in Australia)
– particle physics (WASO in Greece).

And yet, the WASO story is only just beginning.

4 Research Results

The initiative to conduct research about Write a Science Opera began relatively recently. In this section we wish to summarise the findings of two research studies. The first of these focussed on WASO's capacity to motivate pupils. The second concentrated on the kind of creativity which WASO enables, and on improving WASO's educational design (Ben-Horin et al., 2017).

Write a Science Opera has the potential to boost pupils' motivation for both science and arts classes in schools. These results were provided in 2016 following a study of ninety-five Portuguese pupils who participated in WASO activities in Portugal. The study relied on a quantitative research design which implemented Likert-scale questions both before and after the pupils' participation in WASO. The authors did, however, point at the need to further explore two related areas in future research. The first of these was whether or not similar results could be witnessed in higher education. In the second, they called for further knowledge regarding the creative element in WASO, and specifically how pupils could be guided into better handling the creative space which arises in WASO (Volta e Sousa et al., 2016).

The creative character of the process of Write a Science Opera (WASO) may be characterised in various ways. Each of these illuminates various aspects of the complex, collaborative process which pupils undergo during WASO. In a study from 2016, a theoretical approach to creativity which links creative activity and identity building was employed to explore WASO (Chappell et al., 2016). The study found that in WASO, educators and pupils together engage in a collaborative process in which they create a science opera while simultaneously creating a collaborative identity (Ben-Horin et al., 2017).

5 How Much Time Does It Take?

> Time has a wonderful way of showing us what really matters.
> MARGARET PETERS

It is possible to implement a satisfying WASO project within various lengths of time. A typical project lasts for one to two weeks, but you may choose to implement some basic exercises which require only a few hours in order to get a taste of what a more elaborate project might be like for your pupils. Indeed, some groups decide to work with WASO for an entire year. In Chapter 5 you will find an overview of the steps taken in WASO, including how much time each step will require.

6 Can All Children Join?

Yes, all children can join. WASO has been implemented by many schools and with a diversity of groups, including children with special needs. Cooperation is an important part of the WASO process and children typically help each other. During the project there are various kinds of tasks and each child can do something which is achievable or fits them best, even when circumstances change or when there are technical (or other) limitations.

6.1 *Children at Refugee Centres*

Several WASO projects have been implemented with children who live in refugee centres. Language sometimes poses a challenge, as these children often speak different languages than yours. In these cases, we can recommend using gibberish (fantasy language), body language, pantomime, asking children to use their own language, or even using a mixture of languages. The mix is interesting to listen to and, if needed, a narrator can translate and lead the audience through the opera by telling the main parts of the story. The diversity of the children's origins often leads to wonderful choices for scientific subjects. Working with multinational groups also enabled us to realise how diversity can itself teach us many things. For example, with one group we worked on the pre-historic era, which is very different from one continent to another! This might help us to see the world as we experience it from a different perspective.

6.2 *Children with Special Needs*

Children with special needs usually require extra help. In our experience, WASO has proved to be a delightful and successful concept with these pupils. While it lies beyond the scope of this guidebook to provide an in-depth investigation into the various situations implied, we will describe some cases as a source of inspiration.

One group of children with hearing and speaking disabilities created a wonderful WASO project in which they solely relied on sign language: their boundaries led to very creative solutions.

In other cases, groups of pupils which included children with mental disabilities and/or physical handicaps joined WASO projects. This sometimes occurred in cooperation with children without special needs. The way they worked together was inspiring to observe. Typically, parents and other volunteers provided much help. We recommend using the steps of Chapter 6 which describe a process in which the pupils are not required to write or read. A combination of these steps with the ones described in the other chapters is also a possibility. For us, the message is clear: focussing on possibilities always shows a way to enable a genuine inquiry process.

7 Examples of Write a Science Opera Projects

7.1 *The Netherlands*

In the Netherlands, a theatre company (Garage TDI) and an educational company (Speel je Wijs) cooperated to implement a WASO project. The opera's scientific theme was light and the effects of light pollution on humans, our society and the planet. One of the artistic approaches used in this project was shadow play, thus merging the scientific theme and artistic process into a unity. This project resulted in a scene played in the Global Science Opera performance *Skylight*.[2]

FIGURE 8   *Skylight*
PHOTOGRAPH: HENK DE REUS, DE REUS PROJECTS, THE NETHERLANDS, www.dereusprojects.com

7.2   *Portugal*

Curso de Música Silva Monteiro in Porto coordinated a WASO project with ninety-six children between the ages of ten to fourteen years. They simultaneously created four different operas with the same theme: "Earth: A living planet".[3] During the course of five months, pupils developed and improved the opera during their weekly music classes, led by music teachers and primary school teachers. They were assisted by science and theatre teachers. The pupils were proud to perform their science operas at the Casa da Música, a very famous concert hall in Porto.

8   WASO Going Viral: Global Science Opera

WASO recently joined forces with other educational initiatives to create the first operas in history to be produced by a global community.

FIGURE 9 Earth
PHOTOGRAPH: CURSO DE MÚSICA SILVA MONTEIRO PORTO, PORTUGAL, http://cmsilvamonteiro.com/

Global Science Opera (GSO) started out in the spring of 2014 by means of a collaboration between two European Research and Development initiatives. These were the European Commission's CREAT-IT project and the European Economic Area's Write a Science Opera project. The concept of GSO materialised by the pooling together of these previously existing initiatives:
– Write a Science Opera (WASO): developed at the Western Norway University of Applied Sciences.
– The Galileo Teacher Training Program (GTTP) and Global Hands-On Universe (GHOU), two global networks of science teachers.
– Distance Learning: ICT-based connections amongst rural schools, at the Greek educational organisation Ellinogermaniki Agogi.

GSO has developed into a creative education initiative combining science, art, and technology in a global network. Using digital interaction, schools, universities and art institutions from over thirty participating countries perform and live-stream Global Science Opera performances.[4] This is done by inviting a team in each participating country to develop a single scene of the opera, and then performing these together, in sequence: a performance which viewers worldwide can watch on their screens. In addition, local audiences in each country may witness the live performances of pupils in their respective locations. As such, GSO is the first global community opera in history.

The idea for the first Global Science Opera production, *SkyLight*, came about by imagining, literally, a global community making an opera together. Would it be possible? What would the result be? What are the challenges? The idea was proposed to the International Astronomical Union as an official initiative of the International Year of Light 2015.

Since GSO began, the network has developed its own unique understanding of how things work, and why. Schools wish to join GSO productions to experience something new, in a novel and emerging framework, and it offers pupils the experience of performing in front of the whole world!

The educational value has also been documented in GSO, as can be read in the following quotation from Urszula Skolimowska, a participating teacher at Maria Skłodowska-Curie High School in Sucha Beskidzka, Poland, following that school's participation in the 2017 GSO production, *Moon Village*:

> We are proud and happy that we could take part in this venture! It was a great challenge and a great adventure, both scientific and artistic as well as technical ... To sum up, it has to be said that for all people involved in this project, it was blazing trails. We have learned a lot and in many dimensions. So we are an experienced [team] and willing to perform next tasks ... related to Global Science Opera ...!

GSO has produced annual global opera productions based on a variety of cutting-edge scientific themes:
– In 2016, the production *Ghost Particles* in collaboration with CERN, was inspired by particle physics.
– In 2017, the production *Moon Village* in collaboration with the European Space Agency, was inspired by Europe's vision for a future moon village.
– In 2018, the production *One Ocean* in collaboration with the Norwegian Institute for Marine Research, was inspired by the oceans and the need for sustainability in management and use of resources.

FIGURE 10 *Moon Village*
IMAGE CREDIT: EUROPEAN SPACE AGENCY. POSTER BY THE GLOBAL SCIENCE OPERA. DESIGN: JANNE ROBBERSTAD, WWW.GLOBALSCIENCEOPERA.COM

– In 2019, the production *Gravity* was a collaboration with the centennial celebrations of the proof of Einstein's general relativity at Sundy, Principe.

If you would like to join GSO or want to learn more, all information is available at www.globalscienceopera.com

Notes

1 For articles by the Royal Opera House on Write an Opera, consult their website at: http://www.roh.org.uk/news/tags/write-an-opera
2 Global Science Opera, www.globalscienceopera.com/productions/skylight/
3 Supported by the European Economic Area (EEA).
4 Global Science Opera at Wikipedia. Retrieved September 28, 2018, from https://en.wikipedia.org/wiki/Global_Science_Opera

References

Ben-Horin, O., Chappell, K. A., Halstead, J., & Espeland, M. (2017). Designing creative inter-disciplinary science and art interventions in schools: The case of Write a Science Opera (WASO). *Cogent Education, 4*(1).

Chappell, K. A., Pender, T., Swinford, E., & Ford, K. (2016). Making and being made: Wise humanising creativity in interdisciplinary early years arts education. *International Journal of Early Years Education, 24*(3), 254–278.

Global Science Opera. (n.d.). Retrieved January 27, 2019, from www.globalscienceopera.com

Global Science Opera at Wikipedia. (n.d.). Retrieved September 28, 2018, from https://en.wikipedia.org/wiki/Global_Science_Opera

Royal Opera House. (n.d.). Articles on "Write an Opera". Retrieved from http://www.roh.org.uk/news/tags/write-an-opera

Volta e Sousa, A., Ben-Horin, O., Ramos, A., & Teixeira Lopes, A. (2016, March 17–18). Write a Science Opera (WASO): Is there a motivational boost in multidisciplinarity and creativity? In *Conference Proceedings of the International Conference: New Perspectives in Science Education* (5th ed.). Florence, Italy: Libreriauniversitaria Edizioni.

CHAPTER 3

Relations to Multiple School Subjects in the Curriculum

> The illiterate of the twenty-first century will not be those who cannot read and write, but those who cannot learn, unlearn, and relearn.
> ALVIN TOFFLER

∴

The main focus in WASO is on art and science. Yet this approach to teaching and learning naturally lends itself to the incorporation of other areas of the curriculum as well. These could be languages (for example during the creation of opera librettos), math, history, geography, and others. WASO projects may therefore have different, and even tailor-made, learning objectives. As a teacher, you can choose to emphasise more of one thematic subject than another:
- If you ask the children to incorporate at least ten sayings in the performance, more attention will be given to this element of language education.
- If the theme of the opera is the steam train, children will learn more about technology.
- If the opera's storyline is about previous scientific discoveries, history will be a main factor in the process.

In some cases, the learning objectives' focus may shift in entirely different directions than those typically chosen during traditional arts education processes. This occurs due to the need to collect new information regarding the opera's scientific theme. Balancing these provides the core of WASO's transdisciplinary nature.

Furthermore, in WASO pupils typically learn from each other. Provided with enough space to share their experiences, an exchange and cross-fertilisation of acquired knowledge often takes place. In this chapter, we will explain how various school subjects may be naturally included in Write a Science Opera projects within that context.

FIGURE 11   Connecting with other subjects
PHOTOGRAPH: CURSO DE MÚSICA SILVA MONTEIRO PORTO, PORTUGAL, http://cmsilvamonteiro.com/

1   Teaching School Subjects through WASO

1.1   *Language Education*

Creating an opera involves language. Even when creating a performance in which a "fantasy language" is spoken, more traditional language must be involved because you will need language to explain what you are aiming to achieve.

Writing and reading have important roles in Write a Science Opera. (For younger children, we have provided steps without these components, emphasising speaking instead. See Chapter 6.) In WASO, children practice reading comprehension, summarising, distinguishing primary and secondary aspects, and, of course, they generally play with language. They think about dialogues, monologues, song texts, and different ways of expressing themselves. They may use expressions, proverbs, or sayings. During the entire process, children will debate with each other. In doing so, the language skills needed for collaboration will be strongly developed.

> *Tip:* You may even try to create the opera in a completely different language than the one your pupils are used to.

1.1.1   Body Language and Facial Expressions

Body language is essential when creating an opera. In some settings, body language plays a more important role in communication than spoken language does. Just think about it: if someone who is eating a banana says that it tastes good but frowns while doing so, we all know that the banana tastes bad.

In schools, education often focusses on spoken and written language. Allowing more attention to be given to body language may provide valuable and surprising results. If a child knows how to act confidently and is aware of the importance of a proper posture, this can help him or her feel more secure. When one knows how to interpret body language, and practices working on his own body language in an imaginary reality such as a role-play, his skills in this area will be further developed.

FIGURE 12   Expression
PHOTOGRAPH: RIANNE HOFMA, VENSTERSCHOOL, NOORDWOLDE, THE NETHERLANDS

1.1.2   Vocabulary Development

Operas are very valuable for vocabulary development. While children are moving, singing and acting they are necessarily using their senses and experiencing emotions. Memorising may thus be facilitated. An increasing number of studies have shown that movement helps learners focus and learn, including the learning of new words (Smegen, 2014).

1.2   *Mathematics*

Though you might find this surprising, in Write a Science Opera children often employ mathematics. This may not necessarily take place with the pre-planned help of books and calculators, but rather as the direct result of a practical need.

Actors and singers need to find out the distance between them on the stage; the set crew will design and build a scale model and a set; the costume crew will use costume sizes; the lighting crew will discover at which angle and distance the lighting needs to be set and in which setting and colour the play is best accentuated; the children selling tickets calculate prices and revenue and need to know how many spectators fit in the theatre.

It can be interesting to ask the children to reflect on this during or after the process: To what extent did you use mathematics while creating this opera performance? What did you learn? A mathematical problem or subject can even provide the main theme for the opera. In this case, the performance itself will be directly inspired by mathematics.

1.3   *Science and Technology*

Science is at the heart of WASO. All children will explore the chosen scientific theme. Your opera cannot be created before they have established a relationship to that theme. During rehearsals, various questions about science will need further investigation before they can become part of the opera's performance.

Typically, technology is used in abundance. Examples of this are computers used for seeking information, collecting ideas, designing the opera's visuals, and more. Also, other technological devices are used, such as when spotlights are used during the performance. There is a growing variety of exciting digital initiatives and tools that can be used in WASO. Collaborating with a local information technology organisation or your school's science and technology teacher are good ways of exploring this field. Also, online materials may prove to be very useful.[1]

1.4   *Movement and Dance*

During performance and rehearsals, the children will generally be moving more than they would be doing in some other educational contexts. In fact, it

FIGURE 13   Let's dance

would be a good idea to integrate one or more scenes in every opera in which all children are invited to enjoy physical movement or dance. This way, children who decided to choose WASO tasks involving less movement will also need to be physically active. In any case, it is a good idea to have all children participate in the performance at some point.

Obviously, the dancers will be the group that moves most, but actors will move a lot as well. Children undertaking other tasks might also get a lot of exercise, depending on the tasks. For instance, if they are responsible for distributing flyers or posters, or need to visit several places for their investigation, they will be moving a lot.

2   Teaching Creativity and Entrepreneurship through WASO

2.1   *Creativity*

Creativity is important in WASO and, indeed, in all education. Our aim here is thus to support teachers' creative teaching as well as their capacity to teach for their pupils' creativity (Jeffrey & Craft, 2004).

Creativity is not a single, easily defined thing. It may be conceptualised in various ways. It is, then, important to specify what we are referring to when we invoke the term "creativity". A description of the *kind* of creativity which is enabled through WASO's implementation within the school subject curriculum

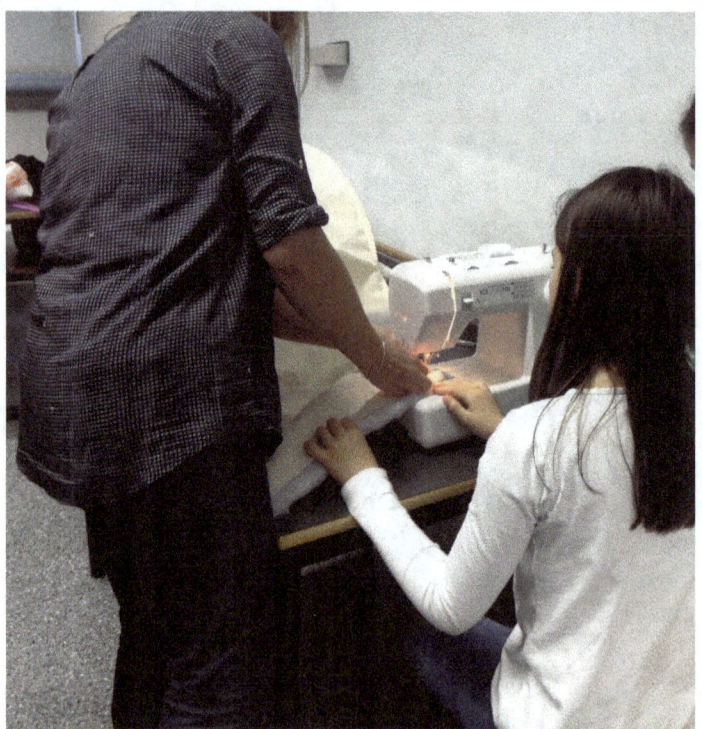

FIGURE 14   Sewing
PHOTOGRAPH: CURSO DE MÚSICA SILVA MONTEIRO PORTO, PORTUGAL, http://cmsilvamonteiro.com/

has been provided by Ben-Horin et al. (2017). The way in which WASO *enables* creativity is described in Appendix 3. Common to both is the renegotiation of what the school subject framework constitutes within each WASO project. Exploring new approaches will offer pupils good chances to develop their own creativity as this will provide them with ample space for their own input and choices. Thinking "outside the box" is vital for this process.

An example: We typically involve theatre, drama, music, visual arts and dance in WASO. But there are no limitations: all art disciplines can become integral parts of a WASO performance. Involving new elements which nobody has used in WASO previously is highly recommended. This can include new ways of approaching the examples provided in this book or a completely new take on the arts' roles in WASO. Pantomime, calligraphy, stand-up comedy and glass sculptures are only some examples of art disciplines which have not yet been involved in WASO. Importantly, WASO's transdisciplinary character implies that involving new art disciplines opens doors for exploring the *science* differently than others have done.

> Creativity is the process of having original ideas that have value.
> SIR KEN ROBINSON

2.2 *Entrepreneurship*

In the twenty-first century, entrepreneurship is considered a valuable skill. There are various approaches to defining what entrepreneurship means, originating from the different traditions and fields of knowledge in which it is implemented. We understand the entrepreneurial mindset in WASO to be the capacity to combine elements and practices from different disciplines in order to solve a problem through the optimal use of available resources and, when necessary, by developing innovative solutions.

We have chosen to include both creativity and entrepreneurship in this section precisely because we understand entrepreneurship as resonating with some of creativity's basic premises. Specifically, renegotiation of boundaries and frameworks are common to both, thus placing pupils partaking in WASO in new and exciting situations in relation to their surroundings. Thus, there can be different ways for the pupils to implement an entrepreneurial attitude in WASO. One way to practice this would be to calculate a budget and have children discover how much a performance will cost and how much money many be gained by means of ticket sales. This could be the task for a group of children, or the entire class could discuss and calculate this. It can be fun to find out how to run an opera business and see whether they could even make money with their performance! Typically, any gains from ticket sales following opera performances are invested in a charity agreed upon by the pupils. Other groups have chosen to finance a post-opera party.

If possible, visit the local opera house or theatre, and make an appointment with staff, in order to provide the children with the opportunity to ask questions about how professional operas combine ideas from various disciplines within the management of a single production.

2.3 *Social and Emotional Skills*

Young people's skills may be understood as divided into cognitive, and social and emotional. Cognitive skills are exemplified by numeracy, reading, scientific literacy, and problem-solving. Social and emotional skills are exemplified by sociability, motivation, emotional stability, working with others, respect for others, resilience, perseverance, self-control, pursuit of long-term goals, will power, self-esteem, discipline and responsibility. Social and emotional skills allow people to translate intention into action, achieve good relations, and achieve better literacies. They can be developed through learning experiences (OECD, 2015).

Children are required to collaborate and experience new situations when they produce their opera. Acting and performing always involve emotions. You celebrate the highlights together and at the same time there will certainly be more difficult moments: when a set collapses, when a scientific question is not easy to answer or explain, when you forget your text, if you don't get the role you would have liked to play, when you feel nervous. We believe that through experiencing and (perhaps) resolving these, WASO provides pupils with a complex, challenging context in which they may exercise many of the social and emotional skills mentioned above. This is largely due to the unexpected relations that materialise between the pupils and their teachers, and amongst the pupils themselves, as an integral part of the WASO process.

Tips: Theatre is pretending in a played reality, making it a safe practice area. Children who are used to taking the lead, and who are often in the forefront, may now find it interesting to play the role of a shy and humble character. The teacher can thus invite children to play roles that are beneficial for their personal development. Another possibility is to ask children to make their own choices and motivate them to specify why they would prefer this specific task or role in the opera's creation. In Chapter 7, "Assigning the Tasks", we will describe these aspects of the WASO process in greater depth.

3 Teaching Sustainability through WASO

> There is no planet B.

In our community, it is paramount that we focus on sustainability. We should inform children about it and teach them how to be critical participants in the efforts towards sustainable development. For example, the pupils' attention could be drawn to our consumer behaviour. Deep ecology teaches us that all life has an equal right to live and thrive, and that we humans are only a part of the big puzzle called life. According to an ecological world view, everything is holistically interconnected.

In WASO we advocate using ecologically sustainable theatre-design, or eco-scenography (Robberstad, 2017). In order to achieve a successful eco-scenography, you need knowledge and skills originating from both the disciplines of science and the arts.

An interesting question could be whether the material (for the set or costumes) needs to be bought (new) or if other alternatives (used materials) could be used, without compromising the artistic process and product. Try to figure out if a stage set and costumes can be used elsewhere once the performances are over, or how the materials can otherwise be recycled.

Note

1 See, for example, www.steameducation.eu

References

Ben-Horin, O., Chappell, K. A., Halstead, J., & Espeland, M. (2017). Designing creative inter-disciplinary science and art interventions in schools: The case of Write a Science Opera (WASO). *Cogent Education, 4*(1).

Jeffrey, B., & Craft, A. (2017). Teaching creatively and teaching for creativity: Distinctions and relationships. *Educational Studies, 30*(1), 77–87.

OECD. (2015). *Skills for social progress: The power of social and emotional skills.* OECD Skills Studies. OECD Publishing. http://dx.doi.org/10.1787/9789264226159-en

Robberstad, J. (2017). *Creativity and ecoscenography in the global science opera* (Master thesis). Western Norway University of Applied Sciences (HVL), Stord, Norway.

PART 2

Let's Go!

FIGURE 15　Let's go!
　　　　　PHOTOGRAPH: RIANNE HOFMA, VENSTERSCHOOL, NOORDWOLDE,
　　　　　THE NETHERLANDS

CHAPTER 4

Warming Up

Carpenters use specific tools, and so do people playing in an opera: their own body and voice are their tools. To correctly develop and use those tools, actors, dancers, singers, and musicians need to warm up. Their body, voice, and instruments have to be prepared to function properly. A warm-up session also serves to get everyone focussed. This is not only necessary before each performance, but also before each rehearsal.

The time needed for warming up may vary, but a warm-up session is always recommended, even before short working sessions.

This chapter gives examples of exercises that can be carried out with your group. For each exercise, the duration, age frame, and required materials are mentioned. Feel free to elaborate with new ideas or variations created by yourself or the children.

FIGURE 16 Warming up
PHOTOGRAPH: CURSO DE MÚSICA SILVA MONTEIRO PORTO, PORTUGAL, http://cmsilvamonteiro.com/

1 Body

1.1 *Loosening Up*
All ages (ten minutes)

Stand straight with your feet slightly apart. Imagine that a string is attached to the top of your head, and that it is pulling you up.

- Let your head drop forward gently and make small turns with your head, first in one direction, then the other. Now raise your head again.
- Roll your eyes: look up, to the right, down, to the left. Make silly faces: close your eyes and mouth as tight as possible, and then open them as wide as possible. Repeat this several times.
- Pull up your shoulders, move them backwards, let them drop, then push them forwards. Do this a few times, alternating directions. Relax your shoulders.
- Move your hands in circular movements, and move your forearms as well so as to move your elbows. Turn in both directions.
- Do the same with only your hands, to loosen your wrists.
- Move your fingers as if playing the piano.
- Put your hands on your hips. Pull your chest up and your shoulders back. Move your upper body to the right, keeping your hips in place. Move your shoulders forward and your upper body backwards, as if being hit in the stomach. Then move to the left and back to your starting position. You are now making turns with your upper body. Alternate directions.
- Put your hands on your lower ribs. Keep your upper body still and move your hips. Move your bottom backwards, then left (bend the left knee), forward, and to the right (bend the right knee). Turn in both directions. Once you can perform this exercise smoothly, you can begin making larger movements by moving your upper body as well.
- Stand on one foot and focus your eyes on a point straight ahead. For younger children, this may be a stuffed toy placed at eye level. Lift your leg and hold your thigh in a horizontal position. Move your lower leg in circles to warm up your knee.
- Hold that position and now only rotate your foot to warm up your ankle.
- Switch legs and repeat.

1.2 *Shaking*
All ages (three minutes)

Stand straight. Pretend to be a drill press and stamp the ground by shaking vigorously (Smegen, 2014). Make small tilting knee movements by bending and stretching them very swiftly. Let your arms hang loose. Your body is shaking up and down.

1.3 *Massage*

All ages (three minutes)

Arrange the group in a circle and stand closely together. Everyone turns to the right, facing each other's backs. Give each other a back massage. In order to make it more playful a theme can be used, for example the weather: draw a sun on your neighbor's back (in circles as large as your neighbor's back). The sun's rays shine in every direction. Clouds are coming: gently push the clouds using your fists. It begins to rain: use your fingertips to make raindrops on the back and head of your neighbour. It even begins to snow! Knead the snow, especially on top of the shoulders, the snow is very sticky. Press your thumbs gently into the shoulders.

1.4 *Mirroring*

All ages (three minutes)

Put on some soft music and have everyone stand in a circle. The first actor starts making very slow movements. All other children mirror these movements. When the first actor points his hand to someone else in the circle, he or she will be leading the movements instead. The others keep mirroring. Continue until the music stops.

FIGURE 17 Watching in the mirror
PHOTOGRAPH: CURSO DE MÚSICA SILVA MONTEIRO PORTO, PORTUGAL, http://cmsilvamonteiro.com/

2 Voice

2.1 Echo Well
All ages (ten minutes)

The group stands in a circle. Imagine that there is a well in the middle of the circle. The teacher starts by saying, yelling, or singing something. The group echoes as accurately as possible. Repeat this several times. Now it is the children's turn. Ask them to decide (individually) what they will say or sing (this can be a word, or even jibber-jabber, gibberish, another language, or a sound). Indicate who will start and in what direction. All sounds are echoed by the entire group. You can provide the children with inspiration for variation by telling them that they can switch between hard, soft, high, low, slow, and fast sounds and echoes.

2.2 Call and Response Song
All ages (four minutes)

This game is similar to the echo well, only now all words will be sung. You can use any words or sentences you like, or even use "nonsense" language. Just make sure it is not too long and has a rhythm and melody. Have the group repeat everything. Keep repeating until the leader or teacher begins a new sentence. If you are in a circle, you can take turns and, for example, repeat every sentence which is sung three times and then continue with the next one. If you like, you can clap, stamp, or snap your fingers while doing this warm-up.

2.3 The Piano
All ages (ten minutes)

The children are in a circle, facing outward, with a "pianist" in the middle of the circle. Have each child think of a sound or a short part of a song which he or she will repeat. They can also clap or stamp the rhythm. The "pianist" presses someone's back (the piano key) and the sound starts. The sound stops when pressing a second time. It is also possible to play various sounds simultaneously. When the "pianist" puts his or her hands on someone's shoulder, he or she becomes the "pianist" and they then trade places.

3 Body and Voice

3.1 Soft Knees
All ages (six minutes)

Stand in a circle. Teach the children the following text and movements:

- Soft knees (bend your knees)
- Aha (stretch your legs again)
- Soft knees (bend your knees)
- Aha (stretch your legs again)
- Our solution to the problem (stretch your arms forward and put your thumbs up)
- Is soft knees (bend your knees again)
- Aha (stretch your legs again)
- Hands up (put your hands in the air and stretch upwards – if you like, jump!)
- Hands down (bend forward and touch the floor)
- Oeh (stand straight and say this to the one standing next to you)
- Ahhh (turn to the other side and say this to the one standing there)
- Ooh (repeat)
- Ahhh (repeat)

Then repeat the whole exercise several times using different styles, for example: like a robot, with jibber-jabber, slow motion, as if very cold, tired, or other improvisations.

> Jibber-jabber (also called gibberish, jibberish or gobbledygook)
> Jibber-jabber is a fantasy nonsense language. No recognisable words are used. Still, the audience will know what the actors mean through their tone of voice, volume, and body language. The term jibber-jabber originated from the author Lewis Carroll and his poem "Jabberwocky" from 1896. The author invented many of the words in this poem. It is about a father warning his son about three animals, one of which is the Jabberwock (Smegen, 2012).

4 Acting Exercises

4.1 *Greeting*
All ages (ten minutes)

Each pupil chooses one of the opera's characters (several pupils may choose the same character). Ask the pupils to walk around in the room while mimicking that character's way of movement. When two of the pupils meet each other, they must greet each other as the characters would. Following this, experiment with different ways of greeting that fit the various roles (such as loudly, shyly, using different accents). Eventually, the entire group plays the same character, following the same assignment.

Tip: This exercise is often used after the opera's characters have been defined. During earlier stages in the process, before the characters have been defined, feel free to invent imaginary characters to inspire the exercise.

FIGURE 18
Greeting
PHOTOGRAPH: PETRA MOEDT,
EMMASCHOOL STEENWIJK,
THE NETHERLANDS

4.2 Dialogue
All ages (ten minutes)

Arrange the pupils in two rows, with pupils standing opposite one another. One row plays one character, the other row plays the antagonist. Choose two sentences from the play the actors will need to repeat over and over. Pick an emotion they will be using. Both rows can also be assigned different emotions, or the actors can freely try out several different emotions.

4.3 Murder Mystery
Ages ten and up (twenty minutes)

In Murder Mystery, the players act as if a murder has taken place. The class needs to do some research. The aim is to find out the profession of the murderer, where the killing took place (crime scene), and what object was used. Choose objects which are not used in real killings, for example: a broom, a piano, an ice cream, etc. Speaking is not allowed.

Have three children wait outside the classroom. The rest of the group thinks of a profession, location, and an object. They will be the audience during this game. The first child comes back inside. The group tells him or her which object, location, and profession were chosen. Then the second child comes inside. Now it is the turn of the child who came in first to act. The first step is to present what the profession of the murderer is. The second child repeats the movements and way of acting and as soon as he thinks he knows which profession it is, they shake hands. Then they continue acting out the crime scene. They both play and shake hands as soon as the second child has a clue. (Being sure about it is not necessary.) The last step is to repeat the same process with the murder weapon. When the second child knows which object it is, he acts as if he takes the object from the first player and 'kills' the first child with it, who acts as if he or she is dying and falls to the floor.

Now, the first child sits down with the rest of the group to watch, and the third child enters the classroom. The second child starts acting: profession, location, and object, following the same procedure. The third child watches and acts with the second child. At the end he or she presents the outcome of the investigation: "The profession of the murderer is ...! The killing took place at ... and as a weapon they used a ...". Often, the guesses are not quite right and it is funny to find out how the misunderstanding started.

4.4 *Names*
All ages (five minutes)

Everyone stands in a circle. Someone starts by saying his or her name and makes a bodily movement. The entire group repeats both the movement and the pronunciation of the name as precisely as possible. The same exercise can be done with the names of the characters and the roles in the opera, such as director, or costume designer.

4.5 *Orchestra Director*
All ages (ten minutes)

Everyone stands in a circle. One child leaves the classroom for a moment. Pick another child to be the 'opera director'. This child starts pantomiming playing an instrument (for example a guitar, drums, etc.). All other kids join in the pantomiming as if they are playing that same instrument as well. The child who was asked to step outside is invited back. He or she stands in the middle of the circle while everybody keeps playing. The director can change instruments

FIGURE 19   Names

and everyone in the circle changes as well, correspondingly. The child in the middle tries to figure out who the director is.

5   Concentration Exercises

5.1   *One, Two, Three*
Ages six and up (five minutes)

　　Work in pairs. One child starts by saying "one", the next child says "two", and then the first one says "three". It starts over and now the other child begins with "one". This goes on for a while. Try finding a rhythm. If this works well, the "two" can be replaced by a jump in the air. If the exercise proceeds smoothly, add clapping their hands to "one", and "three" can be replaced by whistling. The counting can also be left out. Variations are possible using different movements or sounds.

5.2   *Freezing*
All ages (five minutes)

　　All children choose a direction and walk at a slightly swifter pace than normal. It is important that everyone keeps moving. This is done individually, so no one touches anyone. Agree on a sound after which everyone halts and freezes (this is a term often used in theatre terminology). You could use a drum or clap your hands for this. The next time they hear that same sound, everyone starts moving again.

Variation: Put some music on. Everyone walks or dances to the music. As soon as the music stops, everyone freezes. Once the music continues, they can move again.

5.3   *Ho Chi Ha*
Ages six and up (five minutes)

Everyone stands in a circle. There are three movements in this exercise. The first actor says "Ho!", puts his or her hands together, and makes a downward chopping movement. While doing so, he or she looks at someone else in the circle. The second actor makes the same downward chopping movement and shouts "Chi!". The two actors next to her both make a chopping movement in the direction of the second actor and shout "Ha!". After that, the second child can look at someone else, do a Ho movement and shout "Ho!". The game continues by repeating this.

5.4   *Hand on Blue*
All ages (ten minutes)

Everyone walks through the available space at their own pace and chosen direction. The teacher shouts orders, such as: "Hand on blue!" Everyone finds something blue as quickly as possible and touches this with his or her hand. There are many options available to allow for variation, such as using other body parts and colours: "foot on purple", "ear on yellow". Another variation is to move to music, and the order (e.g. "elbow on white") is given as soon as the music stops. When focussing on language development, you can choose more specific body parts, depending on the level of the children: phalanx, heel, jawbone, and so on.

5.5   *Sun and Sunglasses*
Ages six and up (ten minutes)

Without telling any of others, each pupil chooses his or her own "sun" in the group. At the same time, he or she chooses someone else as their "sunglasses". Both are kept secret. Sunglasses protect against the sun. The assignment is that each pupil tries to find a place in which the sunglasses are placed between him/her and the sun. Give a sign (e.g. clap your hands) and everyone starts finding their desired position at the same time. Because everyone is trying to get different "suns" and "sunglasses" to align, it is actually not possible to reach the "perfect" situation. This is not a problem, however, as it will provide funny results.

FIGURE 20   Hand on blue
PHOTOGRAPH: ILSE KRUID, OBS OP 'T VELD, EMMEN, THE NETHERLANDS

6   Cooperative Exercises

6.1   *Love Attack*
Ages six and up (ten minutes)
   Without telling any of others, each pupil chooses another one from the group. When the teacher or an appointed child shouts: "Love attack!", everyone runs as quickly as possible to their chosen pupil and hugs him or her. Repeat a couple of times and then have everyone pick another child before repeating again.

6.2   *Living Machine*
Ages six and up (ten minutes)
   One actor stands in front of the class and makes a repetitive movement and matching repetitive sound. Make sure they can keep doing this for a while. The next actor joins and makes another (different) matching repetitive movement and sound. A third actor joins. Expand until there are six actors, upon which the first one can stop. A seventh actor chooses a spot, makes a movement and sound, allowing the second actor to leave, and so on.

WARMING UP   43

6.3   *Musical Chairs without Losers*

Ages six and up (five minutes)

Materials: a sturdy chair for each child; music.

Place the chairs in a circle, facing outwards. As soon as the music starts, everyone walks around the chairs. Once the music stops, no one is allowed to touch the ground, and everyone takes a seat (feet up) or stands on a chair. The music resumes, some chairs are removed, and everyone walks around again. After the music is stopped, everyone tries to stand or sit on the chairs that are left. Again, some more chairs are removed. Once the music stops, the group will need to make sure that no one touches the ground. More cooperation is needed when the number of chairs gets smaller. What is the smallest number of chairs the group can reach?

FIGURE 21
Two noses
PHOTOGRAPH: PETRA MOEDT,
EMMASCHOOL STEENWIJK,
THE NETHERLANDS

Tips:
- Keep a camera at hand.
- Hoops may be used instead of chairs, with each pupil standing in a hoop.

6.4   Sets

Ages four and up (ten minutes)

Materials: music.

Play the music and invite the pupils to dance freely around the room. Stop the music suddenly. As soon as the music stops, call out an order that combines a number with a body part (e.g. "three knees"). The pupils need to form groups as quickly as possible and put the body parts together in the number that has been called out.

Other examples could be: two noses, thirty-four fingers, eight elbows, twelve heels, fifty shoulders, five bottoms, and similar variations.

References

Smegen, I. (2012). *Speel je wijs: Theater, drama en spel voor taalontwikkeling op de basisschool*. Assen, the Netherlands: Koninklijke Van Gorcum.

Smegen, I. (2014). *Speel je wijs woordenschat*. Assen, the Netherlands: Koninklijke Van Gorcum.

CHAPTER 5

Write a Science Opera in Thirteen to Fifteen Steps

This chapter is intended to be used in classrooms with children who can read and write. Creating an opera using the steps described in this guidebook can take as little as an hour and a half. With one and a half hours of preparation, expect the performance to last no more than a few minutes and be partly improvised. Of course, it is also possible to invest more time. In fact, we recommend doing so. Step fourteen can take as long as you want. Indeed, some groups spend a year working on their opera performance!

These steps are written to guide and inspire. No two operas, or the processes which created them, are ever the same. Feel free to add, skip or change the

FIGURE 22
Let's WASO!
PHOTOGRAPH: CURSO DE MÚSICA SILVA MONTEIRO PORTO, PORTUGAL,
http://cmsilvamonteiro.com/

order of these steps in order to design a process which best fits your pupils' needs. Throughout the process, try to allow your pupils to make as many of the decisions as possible.

Table 1 provides an overview of the steps involved, as well as the minimum and maximum time required.

TABLE 1   WASO in thirteen to fifteen steps

Step	Content	Minimum time required	Maximum time required
1	Choose a scientific subject	5 minutes	1 hour
2	Introduce the subject	5 minutes	1 week
3	Select interesting elements about the subject	5 minutes	10 minutes
4	Choose one sub-theme	10 minutes	15 minutes
5	Thinking of questions	5 minutes	10 minutes
6	Choose one of the questions and write a story about it	10 minutes	30 minutes
7	Read the story, choose a title for it, and use your imagination to come up with its characters	Can be left out	15 minutes
8	Tell the story and create tableaux vivants	10 minutes	15 minutes
9	Presentations	2 to 3 minutes for each group = 15 minutes for five groups	5 minutes for each group = 25 minutes for five groups
10	Voting	5 minutes	5 minutes
11	Developing the characters	Can be left out	20 minutes
12	Role interviews	Can be left out	60 minutes
13	Distribute the tasks	5 minutes	15 minutes
14	In the process	15 minutes	No maximum time
15	Performance	5 minutes	2 hours
	Total time spent	One hour and a half	To be decided

The scientific subject is kept in mind throughout the entire process. The facts need to be correct. Often, more investigation and research will be needed during the process in order to fill gaps in the story.

Tips:
- Keep in mind that the audience is not "just" watching an opera, but also learning about your chosen scientific subject and artistic choices.
- It is important to bear in mind that the opera is about a scientific subject and, therefore, prevent turning science into science fiction.

Step 1: Choose a Scientific Subject
This could be any scientific subject you want to tackle that either matches the interests and experiences of the children or that is aligned with the schools' curriculum programme. It could also be a subject the children are struggling with, in which case creating an opera can be used as remedial teaching: repeating and expanding the subject matter.

If you do not have a lot of time to create the opera, a less comprehensive (and more specific) subject should be picked. If you have an extensive amount of time, a more comprehensive subject can be used. The children can also suggest a scientific subject themselves.

Tip: Have children empty their pockets and look at their contents.

Can you make a connection between those contents and science? Could this connection be used as a subject for your science opera?

TABLE 2   Examples of scientific subjects

	Restricted (specific) subject	**Medium subject**	**More comprehensive subject**
Preschool	Eggs	Birds	Spring
	Boats	Floating and sinking	Water
	Ladybugs	Beetles	Creepy crawlies
Primary school, grades 1–3	Brushing your teeth	Losing teeth	The dentist
	Violins	String instruments	The orchestra
	Skates	The history of skating	Skating at the Olympic Games
Primary school, grades 4–6	Multiplication table of seven	Multiplication tables	Why a carpenter uses multiplication tables
	Toilets	Sewage	Water purification
	Our town/our village	Our country	The world

A fun way to choose a subject with the group is the cherry-split method:
1. Choose a random word. For example, "paper". Write it on large paper or the (smart)board.
2. Choose two words you think of when you think of paper. For example, white and scissors. Write these down as well.
3. Take the two new words and start finding words which are associated with these two. Next, forget about the first word, in order to enable new associations. For example, white: snow and T-shirt; scissors: sharp and iron.
4. Keep going until you have enough words for step #5.
5. Each child gets three sticky notes or bullet stickers in three different colours. For example, green, yellow and white. Each child sticks the green sticker by the word she likes best, the yellow one by the word she likes second-best and the white one by her third choice. Make sure all children do this at the same time.
6. Count which words have most votes and select one.

Step 2: Introduce the Subject
This can be done in multiple ways. Here are some examples:
Let's go:
– Visit places with the children. Go to the park or the forest, visit a museum, a bakery, a local artist, go ice-skating, visit an apartment if most children live in houses or a house if most children live in an apartment, attend a concert.
In the classroom:
– Introduce the subject as you would in any other context.
– Invite an expert, a father, mother, local, or acquaintance. Ask this guest to tell the children about the subject and possibly bring props to show and clarify. In some cases, the teacher or a pupil can be the expert.
– Tell a story, read a (picture) book about the subject.
– Watch a movie about the subject.
– First to sixth grade: ask a pupil or a few children to inform themselves about the subject and present it to the class. This could also happen through a working method that is already being applied in other school subjects, such as a speech, book presentation, or news circle.
– Ask the library for relevant literature about the subject and have the class study the books and find information on the internet. If necessary, the class can be divided into smaller groups. Each group studies a sub-theme.
– Start by using the knowledge the children already have. Sometimes combining all knowledge that is present in the group can add up to a lot of information! After this, it is possible to start with round-table talks in which groups make mind maps. Step 4 describes how this is done.

In the next steps (3–8), the pupils work in smaller groups. Divide the class into 5 (or more) groups. The groups do not all need to be the same size. Each group will receive:
- a large sheet of paper (at least A3);
- markers/pens and other drawing materials.

During these steps, several scenarios will be created. All groups will contribute to all these scenarios. For example, a class is divided into 6 groups. The pupils sit in their groups in a clockwise order from Group 1, Group 2, etc. Group 1 completes step 3 on their sheet, and then gives their sheet to Group 2. Group 1 receives a sheet on which Group 6 has completed step 3. Group 2 completes step 4 on the same sheet that Group 1 completed step 3 on. Thus, as soon as a step has been completed, the sheet is handed to the next group.

We encourage allowing the pupils to always use the sheets created by other groups in order to allow for a more distributed creative process to emerge, and in order to ensure that they all feel ownership towards all the scenarios being created.

Tip: Keep blank sheets at hand in case some of the used sheets are full.

Step 3: Select interesting elements of the subject

Tip: Ask for a minimum or maximum number of sub-themes.

Choose the elements of the subject which the pupils find most interesting to work with. Write and/or draw the subthemes at the top of the sheet.

As an example, the subject "fruit" can have several subthemes:
- a piece of fruit
- how fruit grows
- which fruit grows in which countries
- insects and fruit
- fruit growing on trees and fruit growing on bushes
- sugar in fruit
- what you can do with fruit
- recipes using fruit
- how much fruit do we eat?
- fruit-eating animals

All elements of a subject are relevant. There are no wrong answers. When you are done, move the sheet (clockwise) to the next group.

Step 4: Choose one sub-theme
Ask each group to choose one sub-theme related to the scientific subject. Their choices might have different reasons; they could find the sub-theme funny, interesting, silly, or amazing. They do not need to think about it for too long. If they cannot reach a decision together, they should take a vote.

Now ask the groups to do the following: Circle the chosen sub-theme and write and draw as much as possible about it. Write down everything everyone in your group knows about it. In doing so, the sub-theme becomes the new subject. You may even choose to use a word web or mind map. Once this step is completed, hand the sheet over to the next group (clockwise).

> What is a word web and how is it made?
>
> Write down, draw, or glue a picture of your subject at the centre of a sheet of paper. Draw a circle around it. Around this subject, write down or draw all words linked to this subject that enter your mind. Everything that can be associated with the subject is fine. A word web can be very personal and when making one with a group, it is possible that one word fits for you, while another does not. Everything is possible. Draw circles around each word and connect them to the word in the middle. If you think that one word is linked to another word, you can connect those as well. Together, they will form one large web.

> What is a mind map and how is it made?
>
> Tony Buzan (1993) invented the mind map and explains it as follows: "A mind map is a visual diagram used to record and organise information in a way that is aligned to how our brains function". Write down, draw, or glue a picture of your subject at the centre of a sheet of paper. Around this subject, you write and/or draw the sub-themes. Draw a line or branch to each sub-theme. Smaller sub-themes or less important subjects are drawn as twigs, connected to the branches they are best aligned with.

Step 5: Thinking of Questions
Encourage the pupils to generate questions about the scientific subject-matter. Remember: there are no wrong questions. Write them all on the sheet and ask the pupils to create drawings inspired by the questions.

WRITE A SCIENCE OPERA IN THIRTEEN TO FIFTEEN STEPS

FIGURE 23 Mind map

FIGURE 24 Thinking of questions
PHOTOGRAPH: CURSO DE MÚSICA SILVA MONTEIRO PORTO, PORTUGAL, http://cmsilvamonteiro.com/

Tip: HDY-questions can help to find challenging questions: "How do you …". It might also help to ask "What would happen when …"-questions.

Hand the sheet over to the next group (clockwise).

Step 6: Choose One of the Questions and Write a Story about It
This is the first step in creating the actual opera. This description gives a clear overview of the storyline. It is a summary of the content and does not contain dialogues. In an opera this is called the synopsis.

> Synopsis
>
> The word synopsis is Greek and the literal meaning is "see(n) together".

The synopsis describes:
- what happens in the opera (the main storyline);
- who the main characters are (you might have to set a maximum number of main characters, such as five or six).

During this step it may be necessary and useful to allow time for scientific research in order to learn more about the subject.

FIGURE 25 More scientific research might be needed
PHOTOGRAPH: CURSO DE MÚSICA SILVA MONTEIRO PORTO, PORTUGAL, http://cmsilvamonteiro.com/

Tips for creating the synopsis:
- Start by thinking about what you really want the performance to be about. This is also known as the dramatic conflict. The word conflict often evokes the idea of a fight, but no fight needs to be involved.

> Dramatic conflict
>
> The dramatic conflict is what the performance is about. You can see it as the motor of your story.

- What does a character want to achieve? Which problem or question needs to be solved? Write a storyline based on those ideas and do not go easy on your characters. Little Red Riding Hood would be very boring if Little Red Riding Hood would cheerfully walk to her granny through the forest, they would drink tea together, and she would go home. Add elements to the story that make it exciting or surprising.
- The synopsis needs a beginning: how does the story start?; middle: what happens then?; and ending: how does it end?
- Use WH-questions: What is going on? Who? Where is it situated? When is it happening? Why ...? Whereby ...? Which ...?
- Come up with a main protagonist and think about what he or she will do (or wants to do) in the story. Think of who, or what, he or she will need to achieve this, and how this evolves.

> Protagonist
>
> A protagonist is the leading character. The person who is opposed to this character is called the antagonist. The antagonist struggles against or competes with the protagonist.

Once this step has been completed, hand the sheet over to the next group (clockwise).

Step 7: Read the Story, Choose a Title for It, and Use Your Imagination to Come up with Its Characters

> *Tip*: If you use a fixed number of (main) characters, ask to describe that number of characters. Later on, extra roles can be added for larger or smaller groups so that all the pupils may participate in the performance.

Read the synopsis and find a title for the story. Describe the details regarding each of the opera's characters (age, gender, hobbies, favourite music, food, job, etc.). In theatre and opera everything is possible, so think of animals and inanimate things for roles as well. You could draw or glue cut-out pictures on the paper. What do the characters look like?

Tip: In Appendix 2 you will find questions that can help with elaborating the character descriptions further.

Hand the sheet over to the next group (clockwise).

Step 8: Tell the Story and Create Tableaux Vivants

Tableau vivant

Tableau vivant is a working method often used in drama and dance classes or performances. The word tableau vivant is derived from French. It literally means "living painting". A tableau vivant is a still image formed by several persons using their own bodies to form the image. Trees, objects, or buildings can also be represented by actors in a tableau vivant. The plural is "tableaux vivants", both are pronounced as: "tablo vivan".

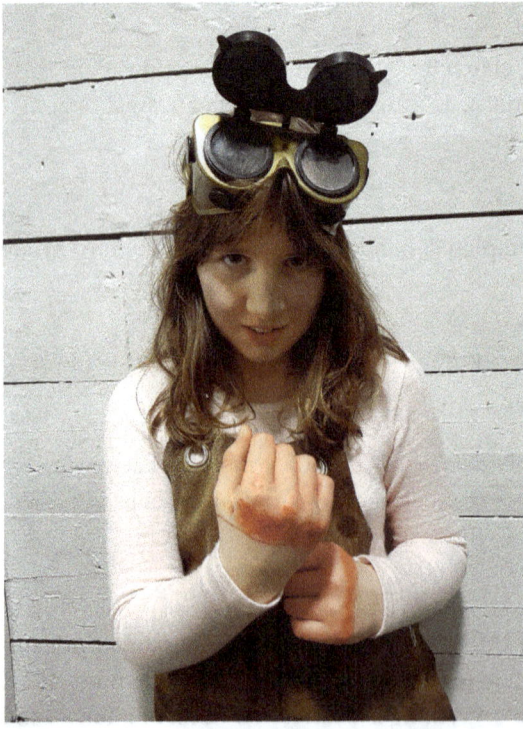

FIGURE 26
Tableau vivant
PHOTOGRAPH: KRISTIN
SALTKJELVIK, NORWAY

Each group reads the synopsis and role descriptions on the sheet they have received. Now, they should practice telling that story and create some tableaux vivants inspired by it, for example at the beginning, middle, and end of the story.

Choose one narrator and have the others in the group act the images. Alternatively, everyone in the group could narrate part of the story, and they all participate in the tableaux. If the group is not familiar with tableaux vivants yet, begin by practising and creating some examples.

The aim of this step is to start thinking about what the three most important parts of the story are. The tableaux can be used in the performance, but this is not necessary.

Tip: Use a large sheet or cloth. Two children hold this up, while the others line up behind it for the tableau vivant. Drop the curtain as soon as they are ready.

Step 9: Presentations
Each group presents the opera scenario for which they have been creating tableaux vivants, for the rest of the class. The presentation by each group begins with the opera's title. All the different scenarios which were created by the different groups should be presented.

Tips:
- Ask the audience (the children watching) to close their eyes or turn around while a group is preparing. As soon as they are ready, tell them they can open their eyes and watch.
- You might want to appoint a secretary who writes down a short description of each story on a flip chart or interactive whiteboard. This is a task you can take care of yourself as well. Alternatively, you can have all children take notes.
- For a fun addition to this step, ask one of the pupils to present his or her tableau vivant in front of the whole class after all the presentations have been made. The other pupils ask the pupil on stage questions about the character or object being represented in the tableau vivant. The pupil on stage then "comes to life" by answering these questions. Examples of questions: "how old are you?", "do enjoy being your character?", "what is the funniest thing that ever happened to you?", etc.

Showing Attention

Take your time to discuss with the children how we treat each other during presentations. This works best if children get their own say on the matter. A

question such as "How do you show respect for the actors?" can be helpful. Sometimes it can be good to make a couple of commitments. Here are some examples of commitments made by children who participated in previous WASO projects:
- The audience is quiet during the play or presentation.
- We put a door hanger outside so that no one will enter the room and disturb us.
- It is OK to laugh about something that happens in the play, but not OK to laugh at the children in the play.
- After the presentation, all actors and narrators take a bow and receive a round of applause. Even if it did not go as planned or you feel that it failed, you will still be applauded. You tried and did your best.
- During evaluations you give more compliments than criticisms. (In some cases, nothing but compliments are given.)

Step 10: Voting
During this step, one of the opera scenarios will be chosen to work with further. Begin by reminding your class that they have all contributed to all the scenarios, so none of them feel excluded in case their favourite scenario is not chosen. Begin by asking everyone to close their eyes. It is important that all eyes are closed, so no one can be influenced by their peers. Everyone can cast one vote only.

Write the titles of the various scenarios on the board, read them out loud and write the number of votes next to the titles. In case of a draw, you can choose yourself (of course, without sharing your personal choice with the group). Alternatively, you can vote again but this time, only the scenarios which received the most points (draw) are voted upon.

After the poll, everyone opens their eyes and the scenario which will be turned into an opera is revealed. Read that scenario's synopsis out loud for the whole class.

Tip: It is possible to use two stories and divide the group in two.

In this case, the rest of the process is done in two groups. This can be done simultaneously, with each group in a different part of the room. However, if you are a first-time WASO teacher we recommend working with a single synopsis during your project.

Step 11: Developing the Characters
You will need several large sheets of paper, thick markers, and scissors. Decide how many of the synopsis's characters will become main roles in the science opera. Explain to the pupils that those who play the main roles are not providing a more important part of the WASO process: everyone is equally involved. Children playing a minor role can take on other tasks as well.

If five main characters are chosen, five children lie down on a large sheet of paper. A roll of wallpaper works well. Other children will draw the silhouettes of the children that are lying down. Once done, they can be cut out. Place the silhouettes next to each other with enough space so that pupils may walk freely between and around them. Write the name of a character on each of the cut outs. Descriptions are also fine (the fairy, the boy, etc.).

Divide the children into new groups, with one group for each silhouette. During the following activities, each group will move to the next character after each question, taking into consideration what is already written or drawn about that character. The steps don't have a fixed order and it is also possible to add other tasks or leave some out.

1. Is the character female or male? Mark the paper with the corresponding symbols.

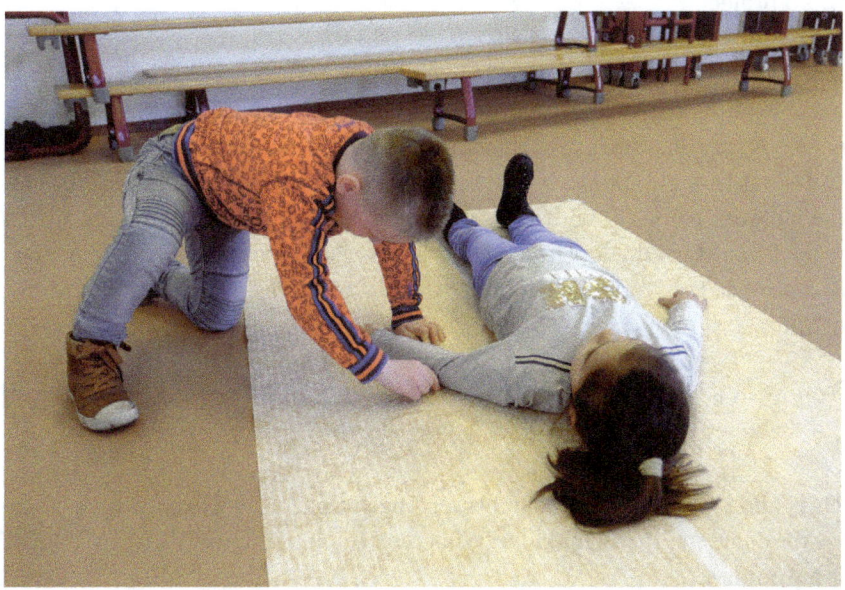

FIGURE 27   Silhouette
PHOTOGRAPH: RIANNE HOFMA, VENSTERSCHOOL, NOORDWOLDE, THE NETHERLANDS

2. Think of two positive features of this character and write them down on the paper.
3. Think of one negative feature of this character and write it down in a different colour.
4. Make two slits in the sides of the body to fold a flap. Write a secret about this character on the back and fold the flap over.
5. Give the character a name. Write it with large letters on the paper.
6. Describe an element of the costume which this character should have. Write this inside the character's body. This can be a colour (e.g. red) or a style (e.g. modern, trendy, old-fashioned, etc.).
7. Describe which music best fits this character. Write this on the character's body. It can also be the name of a song, a music style, a sound, or anything else you would like to include.
8. Think of a profession for this character and describe some of his or her daily activities. Write this on the character's body.

The development of the characters can be short, or longer if you have extra time available.

After this, everyone walks around and looks at the characters. Hang the characters on a wall to make them permanently visible for the duration of your WASO project.

Step 12: Role Interviews
Ask one pupil to take a seat in front of the group and represent the role of one of the opera's characters. All the other children function as interviewers. The child that is being interviewed invents answers to the questions asked. Have the children come up with their own questions and write them down, as a real journalist would do. The goal of this interview is to develop the characters and provide inspiration; the children get to know the characters and invent features.

> *Tip:* A second child can sit on a chair behind the character.

This child represents "the thoughts" or "the brains" of the character. It is a way for the character to ask for help: "What am I thinking?" "How did it go?" "What is my opinion?"

Step 13: Distribute the Tasks
By now, everyone is familiar with the storyline and what the characters look like, so we are ready to prepare the performance. First, tasks need to be chosen.

Think about which tasks you will need. In the following table, we describe recommended tasks which are important for the opera's creation. Other elements can be added and you may choose to leave some of these out, depending on the size of the group, the available amount of time. Also, the expertises of other teachers at your school (e.g. music teacher, visual arts teacher) will prove to be an invaluable resource, so we encourage you to try and engage them in your WASO project.

You can decide for yourself how many children will complete a task (sometimes one pupil can handle two tasks).

Step 14: In the Process
Each group should now be able to start working independently. Motivate the groups to avoid debating for too long. Rather, they should quickly start rehearsing, designing, investigating, organising, and carrying out their tasks.

TABLE 3   Distributing the tasks

Element	Who gets which tasks?	Guidance for number of children in a class of twenty to thirty pupils	Additional information for the teacher
Directing	The director will direct the performance. S/he decides what the actors are to do and what the performance will look like.	One or two.	This is a task you can take care of yourself or give to multiple children.
Assistant directing	The assistant director helps the director and sometimes works with a group of actors. S/he also makes sure that agreements are made between the different groups.	One or two.	
Script writing	The librettists (script-writers) write the libretto (text) for the opera's scenes. They assist the director by making changes to the libretto during rehearsals when needed.	One or two.	This task can also be carried out by the assistant director if the science opera is short and the class is a small one.

(*cont.*)

TABLE 3 Distributing the tasks (*cont.*)

Element	Who gets which tasks?	Guidance for number of children in a class of twenty to thirty pupils	Additional information for the teacher
Acting	The actors act and sing. Often, they will also dance.	Part of the group will play a main role (maximum of ten). Children with other tasks can participate in group scenes.	
Music	The opera's musical score is created by the pupils in the orchestra. This group has two tasks: composing (during the WASO project) and performing the music (during the performance). Sometimes, they may also sing together by forming a choir for one or more of the opera's scenes.	A small group is responsible for the music (maximum of ten). All (or many) children can sing in the choir or play in the orchestra.	Children who did not learn to play an instrument prior to the WASO project can participate by learning simple phrases on a chosen instrument or by using their voices to generate different sounds.
Set designing	The set designers design the opera's set. The set builders build the set.	Two to six.	
Props	Props are objects used in an opera. They are designed, made, and collected by the responsible group.	Two or three.	Set and props can form a single group.
Costumes	The costume designer designs the costumes and makes them.	Two or three.	
Make-up	The make-up artist designs the performers' make-up and does their make-up before the performance.	Two.	

(*cont.*)

TABLE 3 Distributing the tasks (*cont.*)

Element	Who gets which tasks?	Guidance for number of children in a class of twenty to thirty pupils	Additional information for the teacher
Dance	The choreographer designs the dances and instructs the dancers in how to perform those dances.	A small group is responsible for the dances (maximum of ten). But many or all children can participate in the dances.	
Technology	The technicians are responsible for the planning and handling of the technological equipment: e.g. the (stage) lighting is working, the music starts on time. Their role may also be expanded to include light-design if the necessary equipment is available. They will work closely with the set designers.	Two.	
PR (Public Relations)	The PR-group creates publicity for the performance and invites the press and the audience to attend.	Two to four.	
Opera chiefs	The opera chiefs ensure the smooth communication between all the groups. It is their responsibility to greet official visitors as they arrive at the opera's performance (e.g. the mayor or the school's principal).	Two to four.	It is a good idea to ask the opera chiefs to give a short speech before the opera's performance, in which the process leading up to the opera is described.

FIGURE 28 Perform
PHOTOGRAPH: MARIEKE MCBEAN PHOTOGRAPHY, UK, HTTP://WWW.MARIEKE.CO.UK

Tip: For longer WASO projects, arrange interim meetings during which each group provides a short overview of how far they have come so far and what their next steps will be.

These can also include presentations. The meetings can be used to ask each other for help or to give feedback to other groups.

During the process, always check, check, and double check whether the science is evidence-based and factually correct. Ask groups to do more research if needed. It is often tempting to rely on science fiction, but this is not the aim of a science opera. After the performance, the audience should understand more about the scientific theme chosen by the class.

Step 15: The Opera Performance
The children will perform their science opera for their audience. It is recommended to conduct a dress rehearsal before the performance. If you do this one day before the opera's public performance, the children will have time to make necessary improvements.

Tips:
- Ask the audience to turn off their mobile phones.
- In a theatre, flashing cameras can be disruptive, so it might be a good idea to prohibit those. If there is a school photographer available, he or she can take pictures for everyone.
- The children will receive applause. Practice this during the dress rehearsal. Have the actors make a gesture towards the technicians and the other crews behind the scenes, so that they may receive an applause as well. It is also possible to name all groups and ask them to come on to the stage. Make sure that this maintains a certain pace.

Debriefing is important and should not be forgotten. Take some time to give feedback to the group, even if it is late and parents are waiting. This should consist mainly (or only) of compliments. Details can be discussed in school the following day, but the closing comments should always be positive.

Reference

Buzan, T. (1993). *The mind map book. How to use radiant thinking to maximize your Brain's untapped potential.* New York, NY: Plume.

CHAPTER 6

Write a Science Opera in Seven to Eleven Steps

This chapter is intended to be used in classrooms with very young pupils, pupils who cannot read or write, pupils who have special needs, or pupils who do not yet speak the local language. Because young children do not yet read and write, and children with special needs might not be able to, we chose to provide a separate description aimed at fulfilling these needs. These steps for creating an opera are similar to the steps in Chapter 5. You may use that chapter as inspiration and as a reference for your work with this one. You may also find that some of the elements in that chapter are applicable for the pupils described in this one, and vice versa. The following steps are thus not intended as a strict frame, but rather to serve as guidance. Feel free to give them your own personal twist.

Building a set is not included in these following steps. If you wish to add it, you can find guidance in Chapter 5.

FIGURE 29   Let's WASO again!
PHOTOGRAPH: MARIEKE MCBEAN PHOTOGRAPHY, UK,
https://marieke.co.uk

WRITE A SCIENCE OPERA IN SEVEN TO ELEVEN STEPS

Step 1: Choose a Scientific Subject
Any scientific subject can provide inspiration in the WASO approach. Pupils can also make this choice themselves. Examples for this step are provided in Chapter 5.

Step 2: Introduce the Subject
The introduction of the subject can be done in the same way as we have described in Chapter 5.

Some examples that are easy to use: the subject "water", introduced with a water basin that teaches the children how floating and sinking work; the subject "bread", with a visit to a bakery as an introduction; or "plants", introduced by a picture book.

Write the subject in the middle of a large sheet of paper, paste a picture of the subject, or make a drawing of the subject. Children can also do this themselves.

The next steps can be carried out by multiple groups, and are similar to the process described in Chapter 5. The sheets can be passed on to another group after each step is completed. This is only possible if there are enough coaches available to guide all groups. Children from older grades, trainees, teaching assistants, or parents can also be useful as coaches.

If this is not possible, the next few steps can be carried out by the entire group or some smaller groups. Another option is to use alternating groups: while the other children are playing, one small group can take turns working on the opera with their teacher. The first group takes care of step three, the second group of step four, etc. This rotation still allows the children to create the story together.

Step 3: Choose the Elements of the Subject
Have children name elements of the subject they like, or find funny or special. Write or draw these around the subject on the sheet of paper.

Step 4: Choose One of the Sub-themes
Have the children explain to each other why they like a specific element or find it interesting or funny. It is possible to guide the questioning: "Omar, could you explain what you find to be the funniest element on that sheet of paper?" "Why?" "Anna, which elements would you like to know more about?" Voting is also an option. The sub-theme is now elaborated and becomes the subject for the science opera's synopsis.

Step 5: Write down Questions about This Subject
Encourage the pupils to generate questions about the scientific subject-matter. Remember: there are no wrong questions. Write down as many questions as they can think of. Targeted questions can help the pupils: "Who can ask a question to which we will certainly not know the answer?" "Who can come up with a question about …".

Step 6: Choose One Question and Conceive a Story about It
The children can take turns explaining their ideas. Another option is to have each of them come up with a part of the story. Make drawings while the children are speaking. Children can also do this themselves. The meaning of the story does not need to be immediately obvious.

You could also record this story telling as a movie or sound recording. This could then be listened to in step seven. Another option is to elaborate and correct it with the children. The children could make matching drawings for each element and this "book" could then be added to the classroom's reading corner.

> *Tip:* A hand puppet can be inspiring during this stage.

The puppet shows up and is curious about the story. The puppet can ask questions. Who was that? What happened then? Why did he do this? Where were they at that time? What did they do then?

FIGURE 30   The power of puppets
PHOTOGRAPH: MARTINE GOULMY, ALLES CATS, THE NETHERLANDS, www.allescats.com

Step 7: Read the Story a Second Time, Find a Title and Come up with Characters
If a sound recording or movie was made of the story, it is possible to have a look at or listen to it with the group. Come up with a title together with the children. They can also think about the characters. Who does what? Who else was around?

If you use a hand puppet, it could participate here again.

Step 8: Add Music, Dances and/or Songs to the Story
Encourage the pupils to improvise songs about the scientific subject. Invite others to improvise music on instruments. If you need additional inspiration, invite the children to think of songs with which they are familiar. Use the melody and change texts if needed.

Aim to sing parts of the story, which is essential in operas. There will typically be parts of the story to which you can add a choreographed dance or to which the children can improvise a dance. This can be done as one large group, in pairs, smaller groups, or individually.

FIGURE 31 Dancing
PHOTOGRAPH: PETRA MOEDT, EMMASCHOOL STEENWIJK, THE NETHERLANDS

Step 9: Turn the Story of the Opera into a Storytelling Pantomime
Pantomime is acting without speaking. A storytelling pantomime is guided improvisation. The teacher tells a story while the children play this story simultaneously. They all play the same role at the same time, individually, acting without speaking.

Tips:
- Tell the story in the second person. "You are walking outside, watching birds flying in the sky. Now you sit down, because you need some rest". When doing this in the first person ("I am walking outside ..."), you (the teacher) are talking about yourself. Using "you" allows the children to feel more personally involved.
- Integrate enough action but add quiet moments once in a while. ("Watch the birds, you listen to the sound of the sea ...".)
- Tell the story in the present tense. You are playing now.
- It is best to have all children play one character in this step. For example, if you are telling the story of Little Red Riding Hood, everyone plays Little Red Riding Hood.
- Participate yourself and take time to observe every now and then. Acting yourself is especially important when the children are not familiar with all words used.
- If sounds are needed, make agreements on when it needs to be quiet again. You could use a sound to signal that the story goes on (Smegen, 2014).

Step 10: Tell the Story One More Time and Make Tableaux Vivants
Tell the story one more time and have children make tableaux vivants of some elements of the story. Choose the points at which the songs will be added or other sources of music will be used. The rehearsal is important in order to familiarise the children with the story. You could also ask the children to tell the story themselves.

Step 11: The Performance
A simple way of realising the performance could be to combine steps eight, nine, and ten. Children could take turns being narrator, and short dialogues can be added.

FIGURE 32
The performance
PHOTOGRAPH: PETRA
MOEDT, EMMASCHOOL
STEENWIJK,
THE NETHERLANDS

Reference

Smegen, I. (2014). *Speel je wijs woordenschat*. Assen, the Netherlands: Koninklijke Van Gorcum.

CHAPTER 7

Assigning the Tasks

The children will have to choose a specific task. They will be responsible for that element of the opera. Of course, the overall responsibility for the entire opera lies with all the pupils. However, choosing specific tasks will allow the pupils to explore one of its areas more deeply. This third part of the book gives an overview of the available tasks and what they consist of. Feel free to add your own and the children's ideas.

FIGURE 33   Different tasks
PHOTOGRAPH: JOANNE BARTOL, THE NETHERLANDS

1 Directing

The stage director leads the performance through collaborating with all the groups. He or she makes the final decisions. On the one hand, the director is "invisible" to the audience. On the other hand, the director carries a great responsibility. If you have more than one director, it is important that they have the time to consult with each other and make joint decisions. This chapter will give some tips for the direction. Older children and teachers who take the role of director should read this. Many elements can be used both for younger and older children.

1.1 Choice of Style

The director first decides which style best fits the opera. There are many ways to understand "style". Some examples regarding the practical implications of your opera's style: will actors behave very seriously on stage, or in a humorous way? Will some roles be minimalistic and other exaggerated in order to create tension and contrast between them?

1.2 Stage Directions

The director directs the actors as they play each scene of the opera, giving them instructions. He or she also indicates when the chorus will be singing, when a dance will begin, or when a piece of music will be played. Dancers, singers, and musicians will receive stage directions as well. These could be about:

Location:
- Where will the opera performance take place (in the square, on a special location, on a stage, in the gym, ...)?
- Where and how will the audience be seated?
- Where will everyone be on the stage?
- In what direction will the movements evolve?

Example: Play the scene of the opera once more and imagine that you are on a soccer field. Or: Play this part of the scene in the audience in the space in which the audience will be seated.

Timing and Pace:
- Whether the acting should be slower or faster.
- How long the pauses between dialogues should be.

Example: Play the scene once more, but now as fast as possible.

Emotions:
- Which emotions do the actors use while playing a scene?

- Which emotions are used to play a song or piece of music?
- Which emotions are used during the various dances?

Example: Each character chooses one emotion for the start of the scene and one for the ending of that scene. Characters could switch emotions: character A is happy, and character B is angry. Then character B is happy and character A is angry.

Voice:
- How high or low the pitch of a character's will be.
- Whether someone should speak faster or slower.
- Whether an actor should try another voice-type.
- Whether the actors are speaking loud and clear.
- When a text needs to be yelled, sung, or cried.

Example: As soon as the fight in the scene starts, you start whispering.

Body Language:
- What the actors, singers, or musicians do with their bodies.

Example: The entire orchestra is huddled together, as if they are really scared.

Actions:
- Things an actor could do during the scene.

Example: Say your monologue and eat an apple in the meantime. The apple might be sour, or you choke on it.

Text:
- Whether text can be added or removed.
- The language or dialect used, including jibber-jabber or accents.

Example: Think of a "catch-phrase" for your character and use it often.

> Golden rule
> There is a "golden rule" in theatre: Everything that can be acted, does not need to be said.

1.3 *Run-through of the Opera and Dress Rehearsal*

A run-through of the opera is done in order to find issues that can be improved before the premiere performance. During the run-through, try to imagine that an audience is present. You might even come up with new elements for the opera. The director can use several types of instructions and tools, such as:
- Opera: Sing all texts (loud and clear). Opera singers can reach very high and very low notes!

ASSIGNING THE TASKS

- Rap: Act as if the opera is a rap, and rap all texts. Use big movements with your arms, just like real rappers do.
- Use of space: Use the available space to a maximum. It is also possible to play in the audience's space, on or behind the stage, etc.
- Other location: Play the opera in another location, such as the gym or the square. Everything available can be used for the performance (the monkey bars, the swing, …).
- Strange habit rehearsal: Invent a strange habit for each of your characters and add this to the performance (walk on your toes, fidget with your hair, burp, sing a song at random moments, …).
- "Bear rehearsal": Play the opera slower and with big movements, just like a bear. Also use a very loud and low voice.
- "Italian rehearsal": Play the opera as quickly and "over the top" as possible, just like in old Italian films. Less important texts can be skipped for this exercise. Act in exaggerated ways, with wide arm movements, strong emotions, and loud voices. There is no walking, only running. A two-hour play will take a maximum of ten minutes. A ten-minute presentation will take one or two minutes. Often, an "Italian rehearsal" is a lot of fun and generates elements that can be used in the real performance.
- Technical rehearsal: This is a rehearsal for the technical crew. The actors, singers, and dancers do not need to play at full strength (emotions, large movements, etc. are not needed) but proceed with all steps. This helps the technical crew to see whether everything functions correctly and whether the lighting plan works.
- Reverse rehearsal: Each pupil plays someone else's role.

FIGURE 34   Run-through
PHOTOGRAPH: CURSO DE MÚSICA SILVA MONTEIRO PORTO, PORTUGAL, http://cmsilvamonteiro.com/

The dress rehearsal or general rehearsal usually is the last rehearsal. It is a full rehearsal. The set, costumes, music, and all other elements of the performance are present. Often it is done shortly before the actual performance of the opera.

> *Tip:* Invite some people to the rehearsal as a test audience.

Ask for their feedback (with many or only positive comments to the pupils).

2 Assistant Directing

The assistant director is the right-hand man/woman of the director and helps him or her wherever needed. With a larger group of actors and singers, the assistant director sometimes independently rehearses with a smaller group while the director is working with another group. The assistant director keeps an eye on everything and makes sure the agreements that were made are kept. The assistant director also makes sure that continuity is maintained; e.g. if there are two trees in a set, they need to remain there throughout the opera.

3 The Libretto

The opera's text is called a libretto. "Libretto" is the Italian word for "little book". In Write a Science Opera, there are various ways of developing the libretto. You may choose to develop an extensive libretto containing all dialogues, ensembles, monologues and recitatives. Alternatively, you may choose to develop a "loose" libretto based on some important words or phrases which the pupils will use a starting points for the improvisation of a more elaborate libretto on-stage.

> Dialogues, monologues, and librettos
>
> A dialogue is a conversation between two or more characters. A monologue is a longer piece of text sung one actor. Monologues are not always directed at a listener. A character may be voicing his or her thoughts out loud during a monologue.

ASSIGNING THE TASKS 75

FIGURE 35 Working on the script
PHOTOGRAPH: MARIEKE MCBEAN PHOTOGRAPHY, UK,
http://www.marieke.co.uk

The libretto can be written in many different ways. If more freedom is given to the pupils during the opera's creation process, the opera often turns out to be more exciting. However, a more structured and foreseeable process may prove less risky. It is important to plan this according to your previous experiences with the group of pupils participating in the WASO project.

> Scene
>
> A scene is an element of an opera. Books are divided into chapters, while performances are divided into scenes. The scenes are numbered. Typically, a new scene will begin each time one of the following elements changes:
> – location (the play continues in another location);
> – time (the story goes back in time or moves forward in time: one hour later, ten years later, yesterday);
> – action (something new happens).
> Dances, songs, or pieces of music can all be part of a scene, or form a new scene, depending on the aforementioned elements. These need to be included in your script.
>   The Greek word *skena* and the Latin *scaena* mean "stage in the theatre".

TABLE 4   Example of an alternative script design

Title of the opera					
Scene number and title	Which characters, dancers, singers, musicians are playing?	What is happening (very briefly)? (Stage directions can be noted here.) Beginning-middle-end	Which stage set is used for this scene?	How long does the scene last?	Where will everyone be on the stage? (This can be displayed as a drawing.)
1					
2					
3					
4					
etc.					

FIGURE 36   Use the talents in your group
PHOTOGRAPH: YARON BEN-HORIN, ISRAEL

In the libretto, stage directions will be in italics. The scene's location will be specified as well. Below is an example of a more traditional script:

Title: Little Red Riding Hood

Scene one:	In Little Red Riding Hood's home
Little Red Riding Hood:	Mom, I am going to bring cookies to granny.
Mother:	Now that is a good idea, Little Red Riding Hood! Take some oranges and send her my regards. *Worried*: But do take care! There are wild animals in the forest.
Little Red Riding Hood:	Okay, mom! Bye! *Puts on her coat, takes the basket and two oranges and walks out.*
Scene two:	In the forest
Little Red Riding Hood:	*Singing and skipping.* I am not afraid of wild animals, I am not afraid, I am not afraid … *Is startled by the wolf.*
Wolf:	Little Red Riding Hood! *Licks his mouth.* Where are you going?

4 Acting

Actors cooperate with the director and the assistant director (if there is one). The director will tell the actors what to do. The actors can also work on their own much of the time. During rehearsals, the libretto's lines and the acting are rehearsed. It may be a good idea to begin rehearsing these separately, and then simultaneously.

4.1 *Lines Rehearsal*

If you are only rehearsing the lines, it is called a lines rehearsal. There is no need to move; this can be done while sitting down. Lines rehearsals are useful when the roles have not been distributed yet, and everyone can rehearse the lines of any role. You will not always use a complete script containing all dialogues. If a more "open" script is used, the lines rehearsal will need to be partially improvised.

4.2 Moves Rehearsal

During a moves rehearsal, a character's moves are being conceived. Different ways of walking are tested. Here are some examples:
- Pace: slow, quick, varying, tired, dynamic.
- Manner of stepping and standing: legs open wide, X-legs, on your toes.
- Arms and hands: arms relaxed along your body, tense with clenched fists, making lots of movements with the hands or not.
- Head: straight or hanging, moving quickly and looking everywhere, or very quiet and controlled.
- Chest: chest forward and confident, or shoulders forward and hunched.
- Habit or tic: think of something your character often does, like running your hands through your hair, or putting your hands in your pockets.
- Body language: which emotion emanates from this character? Is he or she aggressive, friendly, fearsome, in love, nervous?
- Contact with others: Does the character make much contact with others or not? Some people often touch others during a conversation, others not at all. Experiment and try. The best ideas are kept in mind and used during the following rehearsals.

4.3 Emotions

Rehearse scenes with different kinds of emotional expression. Keep the best ones in mind. It might be interesting to replace some emotions with others and enrich the performance this way.

5 Music

The group is responsible for everything related to music, singing, and sounds. Sometimes the other groups or the director will give them assignments. (Make a song about …, find suspenseful music for the end of scene two, etc.)

Style of Music

Typically, the music group will make decisions regarding the musical style of the opera.

Instruments

Create an inventory of the instruments played in the group and ask whether children who do play an instrument are willing to do so during the opera. Always put the talents of the group to use. Even if the guitar player is not part of the music group, he or she could still play some supporting music during the opera performance.

Children who do not play an instrument can also make music. If no or few musical instruments are available, music and sounds can be made using other materials. Pots, buckets and pans can form a great drum set, a gravel-filled bin that is moved makes a unique sound, and using a funnel does wonders for imitating a trumpet. An orchestra without real instruments can also be a deliberate choice.

5.3 *Composing*

There are various ways of approaching the composition of music in WASO. Some of these may focus solely on rhythm. Others create rhythm, melody and harmony simultaneously. The important thing is to link the music-making to the level of your pupils. No composition is too simple. At the same time, WASO provides a chance of taking a leap and trying musical forms that you and your pupils have never experienced previously.

Exercise 1: Ask a pupil to read the lines of a scene while the others clap their hands to a pulse. Record this and then have all the actors learn to chant the first pupils' rhythmical interpretation of those lines. Then, ask one of the pupils to try and sing a melody to those lines by adding notes to the original rhythmical interpretation.

Exercise 2: Ask a pupil to play a chord repetitively on the piano or guitar. Ask another pupil to try and sing the lines of a scene, using that chord as inspiration for the newly-emerging melody. Record this, and ask the other actors to learn that melody.

> *Tip:* In some cases, existing songs can be used to compose songs by replacing the texts.

Many children are also very capable of thinking of a melody themselves.

5.4 *Musical Terminology*

Below, we provide a short overview of terms that are often used in operas. These could also be used as assignments (e.g. "next week the overture needs to be ready"). You do not necessarily have to use every single element in each opera you will create. The choices made will depend on the aim of the WASO project and the interests and characteristics of the children.

Overture
The overture is the opening of an opera. It typically consists of instrumental music and reflects the atmosphere of the opera.

Interlude
The interlude is a short piece of music or performance that connects artistically between two scenes.

Chorus
A chorus is a group of singers. A small group can also be called a choir. The choir need not be limited to a specific group; pupils belonging to the technical crew could, for instance, participate in the chorus at certain points during the opera. A combination can be made in which the chorus and the orchestra constitute a single group. A chorus can sing but can also make sounds. For example, if the opera has a scene by the sea, the chorus could make sea-like sounds: the wind, seagulls, the sounds of the open terraces by the boulevard. During an opera a chorus can sing as a group, or it could sing parts of an aria or of a song sung by an ensemble.

Aria
In opera, a song sung by one character is called an aria. An aria displays the emotions or feelings of the character at that particular moment.

Rap
A rap is different from a song. In some age groups, children prefer rapping to singing. Give them this freedom if they need it.

Duet
A duet is a song sung by two singers. Often, they will both sing one part as a solo, and sing one part in unison or two-part harmony.

Ensemble
An ensemble is a group of three or more singers.

Recitative
A recitative is a sung section which is more like a conversation in which part of the story is being told. Recitative often uses the rhythms of normal speech.

Leitmotiv
A leitmotiv is a melody that is played each time a specific character appears. It functions as a kind of signature tune. This could be used for the main characters.

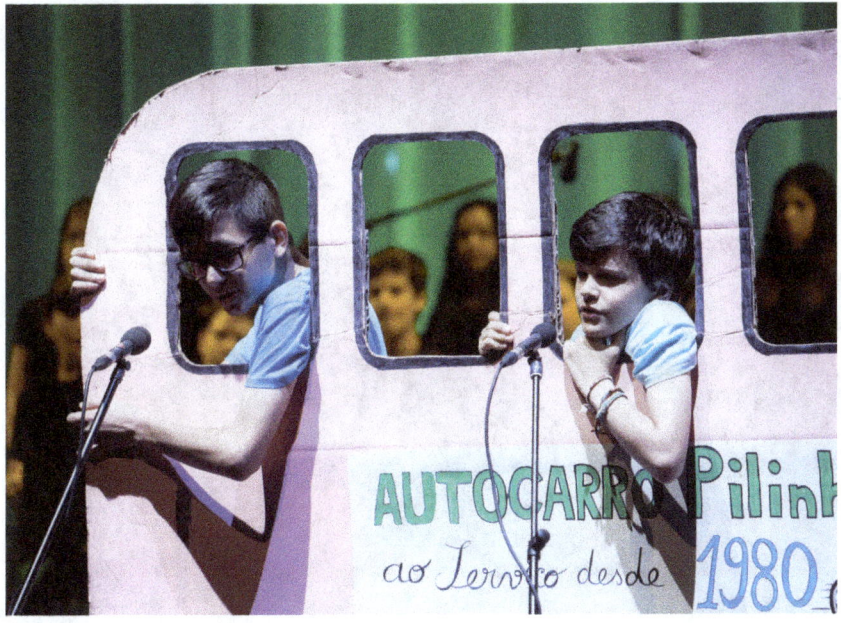

FIGURE 37 Passengers duet
PHOTOGRAPH: CURSO DE MÚSICA SILVA MONTEIRO PORTO, PORTUGAL, http://cmsilvamonteiro.com/

6 Set Designing

The set's goal is to invite the audience into a visual universe in which the story takes place. The set helps the audience and the actors get a feeling of the mood and of the physical, psychological, and/or historic site of the story. The set designing crew takes care of the visual image that is created for the audience. Together with the director and costume crew they select a certain style. Then they start brainstorming by, for example, discussing, making a drawing, or painting. As soon as a plan is agreed upon, the set crew will start making models. This will be a dollhouse-sized set.

Officially, a model should be made on a certain scale. Shoe boxes are handy. If time allows it, the set crew can create several models and the group and director vote on which design will be used for the opera.

Some schools choose to paint the set's curtain. This can be interesting, but there are also many other options. Look at pictures on the internet, or explore opera and theater books at the school's library, in order to get ideas for how professional theatre companies organise this.

FIGURE 38   Less is more

It is important to establish what the main message of the opera is. The saying "less is more" is often true for a set as well. Sometimes a set using five chairs can be more interesting than a complete living room which contains many details and features.

6.1   *Sustainability*

It can be interesting to try and build the set using already available material or material that would be thrown away. The same goes for the costumes; can the clothing be re-used? Can items be found at the thrift shop? Is it possible to use materials that can be used more than once?

7   Props

The group taking care of the props starts making an overview of what is needed for the opera. The actors/singers and the director could also compile a list of what is needed. This list usually changes during the rehearsals, as sometimes props are no longer necessary or other items are added. The props crew assembles everything that is needed, but others can be involved as well. Ask questions during a meeting: "Who has a sledge and can bring it with them?" "Who wants to make the gnome's walking stick?" Some of the props are made by the props crew. If needed, the props crew can place the items at the right spot in the right moment during the opera.

8 Costumes

A costume tells the audience who the character is. Everything should be carefully chosen: the clothes, the materials used, how it is worn, the matching props. The stylist needs to decide on a style for the costumes as well. If it fits the opera, it is possible to unify all costumes by using one matching style. The costume crew could look up pictures for each character or make their own drawings or paintings, and then use those examples to make a choice. The costumes should aim to either be in harmony with the set or form a contrast with it. For example, if there is a lot going on in the set, the costumes might be frugal and simple. The costume crew also decides on the clothes worn by the orchestra and the chorus, and can tell them to look for certain pieces of clothing, hats, or masks.

FIGURE 39
Well-chosen costumes
PHOTOGRAPH: NIRITH
BEN-HORIN, ISRAEL

9   Make-Up

The make-up crew will do the make-up of everyone who is on stage. If the group is big, they will take care of the main characters and give instructions to the others. For make-up, what matters is that the characters and their features are easily recognisable. When using a large room with theatre lighting, all actors need to have some eyeliner and lipstick. If the room is very big, it is a good idea to put some darker foundation on the sides of the nose. Otherwise, the faces will seem flat as the depth falls away because of the lighting. Often the lighting is so harsh that foundation is needed. This can be applied by using a small make-up sponge and should use foundation that is somewhat darker than the person's skin colour. Make-up should also be applied to the neck, ears, and throat, up to the neckline of the costume.

FIGURE 40   Princess doing her make-up
PHOTOGRAPH: MARIEKE MCBEAN PHOTOGRAPHY, UK,
http://www.marieke.co.uk

ASSIGNING THE TASKS

The make-up crew also needs to select a certain style. The make-up can be natural or very expressive and lavish. The make-up needs to match the costume, and vice versa. The make-up crew should draw a proposition for the faces of all characters, showing all make-up, including hair and nail polish. The make-up crew makes sure there is enough make-up and that make-up remover tissues or washcloths and soap are available after the opera. If children bring their own materials, the make-up group will instruct them. If they do not bring their own eye makeup (mascara and eyeliner), for hygienic reasons it is important to instruct them on how to clean the tools before the next person uses them. This is especially difficult with mascara. Unfortunately, it is very easy to transmit eye infections with eye make-up, which is why one should always have one's own.

10   Dance

The dance crew is responsible for the movement and dancing during the opera. If an actor needs to dance, the dance crew will design the choreography. Alternatively, the dance group can carry out all dancing. Sometimes the dance crew will work independently. Other times, the director or group may have specific questions or requests for the dance crew. The dance crew will note if there are children who have dancing experience. This could be used to improve the opera.

FIGURE 41   Let's dance again!
PHOTOGRAPH: CURSO DE MÚSICA SILVA MONTEIRO PORTO, PORTUGAL, http://cmsilvamonteiro.com/

The dance crew chooses a style together with the director. Will it be all ballet or breakdance? Will different dance styles be combined to create a colourful mix? Think of what fits best with your opera. A contrast might be interesting. A modern piece and some ballet can form a very powerful contrast.

The dancers work closely together with the musicians. The musicians need to provide the music for the dances.

The dancers can decide on movements and motions. There might be no music involved. For example, during a scene on the moon, everyone is moving in slow motion from the space station to the flag. The dancers can design the choreography for that scene and dance it themselves, or give ideas and instructions to other actors or dancers.

11 Technology

The technical crew keeps an inventory of all technical needs and takes care of this. This could be anything, from hoisting up a bucket during the opera, to making a PowerPoint presentation that will be shown during a song.

If lighting is used, the technical crew designs a lighting plan, makes notes of this in the script or in a drawing, and then carries it out. The technical rehearsal is very important for this group; they need to test whether everything works properly.

FIGURE 42 Shadow play
PHOTOGRAPH: CURSO DE MÚSICA SILVA MONTEIRO PORTO, PORTUGAL, http://cmsilvamonteiro.com/

ASSIGNING THE TASKS

11.1 *Light*

If you are playing in a theatre, the opera performance will start by switching off the lights in the audience and switching on the lights on stage. Most performances end with a blackout. All lights are extinguished. Then all lights are switched back on and the actors come to the stage to receive applause. Another blackout follows and the lights in the audience are switched on.

When using real theatre lighting, the technical crew needs to design a lighting plan. This gives an overview of which lights are on at which time and when there are changes. In the most up-to-date light panels, the settings can be entered into the system and the next lighting setting can be switched on by pressing a button. If the opera is played in a theatre, the technical crew should

FIGURE 43　Mysterious light
　　　　　PHOTOGRAPH: CURSO DE MÚSICA SILVA MONTEIRO PORTO, PORTUGAL,
　　　　　http://cmsilvamonteiro.com/

make agreements with the theatre's lighting team who will help design the lighting plan. If the performance of the opera is in a school, the technical crew will take care of appropriate lighting. This could be done using construction lamps and Christmas lights. You may also have access to a movable spotlight. The lighting technician needs to know the play, so s/he knows where to move the spot at all times.

12   Public Relations

The PR-crew takes care of all communication with the (potential) audience and takes care of publicity. They design and make posters and flyers and distribute them. The PR-crew invites the audience, designs a website, writes an article for the school newsletter, invites the press, writes their own press releases, and takes pictures. Some children in the PR-crew could also create a 'Making of'. This would show the entire process and picture all crews. For this, many forms can be used, e.g. a written report, a wall newspaper, a film, a blog or vlog (video-blog).

13   Project Management

The children responsible for the project's management make sure that everything gets organised. This can mean many things:
– Make sure that the stage is available at the time of the performance. (Reserve the space.)
– Build a stage, put up chairs or benches for the audience.
– Arrange for someone to make a video and take pictures of the opera.
– Arrange for drinks during the break. If needed, buy and prepare these.
– Arrange for enough microphones to be available.
– If tickets are sold, this is also a task for them: make or buy tickets, deal with reservations and have someone at the till during the performances.
– During the opera performance:
– Ticket sales or checks.
– Let the audience in and show them where to sit.
– Give a special welcome to important visitors and if needed, reserve chairs for them.
– Have the audience write in a guest book.
– Ask the audience to turn off their mobile phones.
– Arrange for flowers for all collaborators after the performance and hand these over.

FIGURE 44　Don't forget the flowers
PHOTOGRAPH: CURSO DE MÚSICA SILVA MONTEIRO PORTO, PORTUGAL, http://cmsilvamonteiro.com/

CHAPTER 8

Extras to Think of When Performing

1   Safety

Safety is an issue that needs to be addressed. For a small school presentation there are not many changes compared to a normal school day, so this does not require much extra attention. For a large performance, it does. This task could be assigned to a specific group or it could be an additional task for another group. This is also a task that concerns everyone, as everyone needs to know what must happen in case of emergency. An element that is often overlooked when thinking of safety, is taking care of yourself as well as each other. Nerves can dominate someone; they might have lost their voice, have a stomachache because of the stress, or have forgotten an important element of the costume. Part of creating an opera consists of helping each other and jointly looking for solutions, for everyone to prosper and enjoy.

FIGURE 45   Think of ...
PHOTOGRAPH: CURSO DE MÚSICA SILVA MONTEIRO PORTO, PORTUGAL, http://cmsilvamonteiro.com/

2 Preparations

Before the opera performance starts, you need to make sure that:
- All cables are taped to the floor so nobody will trip.
- Only heat resistant light filters are used, preferably real theatre lighting filters.
- A fire extinguisher is at hand and that everyone knows where it is; for larger venues more fire extinguishers are needed.
- Consider conducting a fire drill, so everyone knows where to go to when something goes wrong.
- No candles or fire are used.
- The maximum audience allowed into the theatre is checked and that this number is not exceeded.
- When it is hot, check whether the air conditioning is working and make sure that there is sufficient ventilation.
- If the theatre is dark, make sure that some spots in the backstage area are lit to make sure that it is safe to move.
When in doubt, consult specialised authorities.
During the performance of the opera:
- In case of long performances, you need to make sure that everyone has a water bottle available.
- If the theatre is dark, it is useful for each actor to have his/her own small flashlight.

3 Stress Less

> Stress is not what happens to us. It's our response to what happens and response is something we can choose.
> MAUREEN KILLORAN

To relax is not always an easy task for children during the performance or even during the process:
- Some children do not like being in the spotlights.
- Probably not everyone will be doing his or her preferred task.
- Sometimes it does not work out the way you intended, and you are unhappy with the final outcome.

These are all elements that can increase tension. Still, you need to work together. It is important to give this enough attention, and the teacher plays an important role in this. Giving the children the space to share their frustrations could be enough. This might also help them find solutions or make changes. Children can help each other finding these.

> A compliment is verbal sunshine.
> ROBERT ORBEN

FIGURE 46   You are beautiful
PHOTOGRAPH: CURSO DE MÚSICA SILVA MONTEIRO PORTO, PORTUGAL, http://cmsilvamonteiro.com/

It is very effective to have children compliment or thank each other during the process. If you think that some children will not receive many compliments, consider doing the following: write all names on pieces of paper, distribute them among the children, and have them come up with a compliment for the name they picked. Even if it does not always work out the way you wanted to, a compliment is useful to point out that you are doing something well and that other parts do work out. This might be helpful to promote more positive energy.

It can be a good idea to do relaxation exercises with the children, teaching them how to relax their bodies and move away from negative thoughts about themselves, the others, what is being created, or frustrations, fear, etc. One example of such an exercise is the spaghetti exercise outlined below, which takes about three to ten minutes.

Everyone gets a piece of raw spaghetti. Look at and feel the raw spaghetti. Now do the same with cooked spaghetti. (Or talk about it.) Sometimes you feel tense or nervous and some muscles in your body tense up, so your muscles are just like raw, hard spaghetti. Instead, try to relax your muscles like cooked spaghetti. That is what we are going to practice.

– Lie down on your back. Lay your arms next to your body and close your eyes.

- Feel how your breath makes your body move.
- The next time you breathe in, tense the muscles in your left leg. Breathe in and hold your breath for a while. You can raise your leg a little bit. Your leg is raw spaghetti, completely tense, stretched out and hard.
- Breathe out and let your leg lie down relaxed again. Keep breathing. Your leg is now cooked spaghetti, completely soft and relaxed.
- What are you feeling? Do you feel calm or tense, is your leg warm, cold? Whatever you feel, it is all okay.
- Now do the same thing with your right leg. Breathe in, hold tight and tense, breathe out and relax.
- Breathe in: hard spaghetti; breathe out: cooked spaghetti.
- Now do the same with your torso, bottom, tummy, chest, and back. Tense your muscles, hold your tummy in, pull your back up a little ... and relax. Everything is tense like hard, raw spaghetti, and relaxed again like cooked spaghetti.
- Now tense up your left arm and breathe in.
- Breathe out and let it relax. Spaghetti arm hard, spaghetti arm soft.
- Do the same with your right arm.
- Now tense up all the little muscles in your face, squeeze your mouth and eyes together and make them as small as you can. This is your raw spaghetti face.
- And relax. Let go completely, just like cooked spaghetti, completely soft.
- How does your body feel now? Whatever you are feeling, it is all okay.
- Now feel again how your breath lets your body gently move. Feel your tummy or chest go up and down.
- Relax all the muscles in your body. Relax completely, like cooked spaghetti (Smegen, 2018).

4   Making Mistakes

> Failure is simply the opportunity to begin again, this time more intelligently.
> HENRY FORD

An important element in Inquiry, and in learning in general, is making mistakes. Mistakes are important in order to obtain improvements. People who make no mistakes are unlikely to try new things. Inquiry leads to new things; therefore, it is important to learn that making mistakes and failing is part of life and actually helps us.

If you make mistakes, you will learn what does not work. You will discover that you will need to "tweak" things or find other, new, solutions. It is essential to not be afraid to make mistakes, and it is our task as teachers to stimulate children to do avoid being afraid. Children need to learn that failing and making mistakes are crucial parts of the learning process.

We need courage to make mistakes. Sometimes it is necessary to take risks and choose options that are less safe.

During evaluations you could ask questions like: "What is the best mistake you made today?" "What did this mistake teach you?" "What did you do afterwards?" and give compliments about mistakes: "Wonderful, you failed with … and learned that …".

5   Asking Questions

For the learning process, asking the right questions is often more effective than simply giving children information, answers, or solutions. Questions lead to (new) investigations, insights, conclusions, answers, and questions. Questions will take you a little further. This will also teach children how to ask better questions.

FIGURE 47   Don't ever be afraid to ask a question
PHOTOGRAPH: CURSO DE MÚSICA SILVA MONTEIRO PORTO, PORTUGAL, http://cmsilvamonteiro.com/

Reference

Smegen, I. (2018). *Mindful at school: 52 playful mindfulness exercises with kids*. Orvelte, the Netherlands: Speel je Wijs.

CHAPTER 9

Evaluation

Evaluation is a permanent element in WASO. The group will regularly meet, the sub-groups will report what happened and share future plans. At the same time this is the perfect opportunity to ask questions and give feedback to each other. The sub-groups also have their own evaluations, which are not always planned.

This final chapter gives examples of the various evaluation options and how often these are needed.

FIGURE 48 Helping each other grow
PHOTOGRAPH: CURSO DE MÚSICA SILVA MONTEIRO PORTO, PORTUGAL, http://cmsilvamonteiro.com/

1 Frequency

It is a good idea to plan evaluations during the process. How often these are needed or useful depends on the length and course of the process. If you are working for one full day, two moments can be selected during which everyone can meet. If you are working for an entire week, evaluations could happen once a day, and if you are working for an entire year they could happen once a month.

2 Objective of the Evaluation

During evaluations it is important for the children to know that they can freely give their opinion. As a teacher you play a meaningful role in this; the children need to feel secure enough to say anything. Even if children might react badly to the feedback of others, teachers must take care that this is handled well, stopped, and explained why this is not the intention. Each child has the right to give his or her opinion.

Teach children how to give each other constructive feedback, for example by explaining their opinion. ("I did not like the rehearsal on Monday because the music did not start at the right time".) The child or the others can think of ways to solve this before the next attempt.

If you are working with older children, you can take notes. This can be done with younger children as well, using drawings or emoticons.

The objective of the evaluation is to gain insight into how you, the others, and the group function together. Together you are thinking of what can be improved. This will teach you how processes work and will, in the end, improve the general communication and collaboration.

3 Other Ways of Evaluating

3.1 *Making Statues*
In this exercise, children work in pairs and choose a "statue" and a "sculptor". The sculptor will place the statue in a certain position by touching it with his hands; an example may be to lift the arm and spread the fingers. It is important to give the statue a position that can be held for a long time. (Standing on one leg for a long time can be difficult). You can also have the sculptor make a facial expression which needs to be imitated by the statue. You might choose to play some music while the children perform this exercise. However, it is nice to

have them do this in silence. The silence impacts the atmosphere in an interesting way, and postpones the actual discussion until later.

First, half of the group acts as a statue, after which they switch places. Children can choose their own partner or you can let chance decide who works with whom (see Appendix 1 for ideas to split up groups).

Different tasks can be given, and the sculptor explains them as soon as the statue is ready. Here are a couple of examples:
- Make a statue that clearly shows what the most important task of the other person was during this project.
  - ➢ Explanation: Explain what the other person did and compliment him or her.
- Make a statue that shows what you think the other person thought about this project.
  - ➢ Explanation: Tell which emotions you frequently saw. The statue can confirm whether this is true and give a further explanation.
- Put the statue in a position in the group where he or she was mostly present. Choose a position that fits according to you. Maybe a bit outside of the group, or in the middle of it? One position is not necessarily better than the other.
  - ➢ Explanation: Explain why you are putting the other person in that position. The statue is free to react to this.

3.2 Collage, Mind Map, or Wall Newspaper

A collage is an assemblage of different photographs, pictures, coloured paper, or cloth, which together form a new picture. Mind maps were explained in Chapter 5. A wall newspaper is similar to a regular newspaper with the exception of it being displayed publicly on a wall. It has a subject and subtitles, the regional page has regional news, the sports page has sports news, just like a regular newspaper.

These could be made by each group or individually. Make an image that shows what you have done, what you have learned and how you have experienced the process. Different techniques can be used: cutting, pasting, painting, writing, drawing.

3.2.1 Scene
Play a scene that shows what you learned and how you experienced it.

3.2.2 Poem
Write a poem explaining the following subjects: ... (You could also use the questions in Section 9.4.)

3.2.3 Prezi, Film, Stop Motion or PowerPoint

Select a digital format explaining the following subjects: ... (You could also use the questions in Section 9.4.)

4 Final Evaluation

We strongly advise that the children give feedback at the end of the process. With younger children this can be done by simply talking about it. If there is extra help in the group, this could be done individually. The discussions can be taped and used later. Films are also a good tool. Another possibility is that the younger children make a drawing you then discuss with them. Pictures or movies of the opera can help them recall what happened. Ask what they can say about it and how they experienced it.

Older children could anonymously fill out an evaluation form. This leads to new insights and gives them more freedom to express their real thoughts. Possible questions would be:

– How did you experience doing this project?

  I thought it was:
  ○ too difficult
  ○ quite difficult
  ○ perfect
  ○ too easy

– How motivated were you to participate?

  I was mostly:
  ○ not motivated at all
  ○ somewhat motivated
  ○ motivated
  ○ very motivated

– What could be changed to motivate you more?
– What did you like best? Why? Was there anything else you liked? What? Why?
– What did you not like? Why? Was there anything else you did not like? Why?
– What was difficult? Why? Was there anything else that was difficult? Why? What was easy? Why? Was there anything else that was easy? Why?
– What inspired you? Why? Was there anything else that inspired you? Why?
– What did you enjoy? Why? Was there anything else you enjoyed? Why?
– What helped you to learn the most?
– What was different about this way of learning compared to other assignments in school? Can you explain this?
– What would you do differently if there were a next time and why?

EVALUATION

FIGURE 49 Add happiness to your world each day
PHOTOGRAPH: RIANNE HOFMA, VENSTERSCHOOL, NOORDWOLDE,
THE NETHERLANDS

APPENDIX 1

Ways of Making Groups

1. Cut different postcards into pieces. If you want groups of three, you cut them into three, for groups of six you will need six pieces. Distribute the pieces. The children with pieces from the same postcard form a group.
2. Have the children form a row, for example according to height, shoe size, the distance of their home from school, age, or hair length. Divide the group starting from these criteria (the first three, the next three, etc.)
3. The children walk around, you shout a task and they need to form groups as quickly as possible. For example, make a group of:
    - three children with as many brothers and sisters as you
    - five children who have the same pets (or who have no pets)
    - two children that celebrate their birthday in the same month
    - two boys and two girls
    - three children with the same hobby
    - six children with eyes/hair of the same colour
    - four children with trousers of the same colour
    - three children with the same shoe size
    - five children of the same height
    - two children of whom the name starts with the same letter

   Do this as fast as you can!
4. Make cards to divide the group. For groups of three children, you need three equal cards, for groups of four, four equal cards, etc. Each child receives a card and the game begins. Examples of what you can put on the cards:
    - Song titles the children know. Count to three and everyone needs to sing the song simultaneously. Everyone starts looking for the child who is singing the same song.
    - Animals. For younger children, you can print pictures. When the signal is given, everyone plays the animal on the card. Find your own kind. Variation: Make the sound of the animal on the card and find your own kind.
    - Emotions. Use emoticons or describe emotions. Play your emotion and find someone who is experiencing the same emotion.
    - Mathematical problems and solutions. Each problem goes looking for his or her answer and vice versa. For larger groups couples can be put together. Alternatively, two or three problems with the same solution could work together.

- Letters, written in different ways.
- Examples of items that match, according to the subject, such as:
  - Geometrical forms: square items, triangles, round items.
  - Food: fruit, vegetables, dairy products, candies, drinks.
  - Animals: birds, insects, mammals, fish, amphibians.
  - Housing: houses, apartments, houseboats, farms.
  - Topography: countries in Europe, Africa, North-America, South-America, Australia; cities and villages in a county.
  - Cartoon characters or fairy tales: Donald Duck and his cousins, the piglets, the dwarfs, etc.
  ➢ When using cards for the first two options, it can also be done with the eyes closed. This adds another dimension to it.

5. Food: Buy something edible of different colours, for example different kinds of cherry tomatoes. Each child receives a tomato and finds his or her match. As soon as the group is complete, they can sit down and eat. Different kinds of food are also an option. (Bananas, apples, clementines.)
6. Food: Buy apples in different sizes and colours. Cut them into the required number of pieces. Each child receives one piece and needs to find the other pieces of their apple. Once they are ready, they can enjoy their apple.
7. Stickers: Put stickers on the foreheads of the children without showing them what kind of sticker it is. The children will have to try and find out who has the same sticker by asking questions. Variation: Have the children discover their sticker without talking in order to form groups.
8. Picking a string: Cut a piece of string for every two people. Put all the strings in a star formation on the floor or a large table. Everyone grabs the end of a string. The children holding the same string form a pair. If you are using strings with different colours, the colours could also be a match.
9. Lucky dip: Fill a box with different objects of which you have several in your classroom. (Pencils, erasers, blocks, tape, paper clips, rubber bands.) Children with the same object form a pair. Variation: The children close their eyes. They receive an object, open their eyes, and form groups with children holding the same object.
10. Dancing: the children can move freely to the music. If the music stops, they freeze. Repeat a couple of times. The last time, you form groups of children who are the closest to each other.
11. Jump: the children line up and everyone has to close their eyes. Count from one to three. At three all kids either jump to the right, to the left, or stand still. Now you have three groups.

12. Right hand, left hand: Ask the children to close their eyes. Then count to three. At three all children raise their hands, left or right. After this you can divide them in two groups. One or both groups can do the same again to make three or four groups.

APPENDIX 2

Role Descriptions

When describing a role, everything depends on the amount of time available and what you want to describe. The story will also determine what the most important information is. These are a few questions that could be answered. Descriptions do not always need to be written down. They can also be used for a role interview and many elements can also be drawn or painted.

Basic information:
- Is the character a man, woman, boy, girl, animal, thing, or creature?
- Name?
- Age?

Living:
- Where does the character live? In which country, village or town, what landscape, in a house, a boat, a flat, a nest, a cave?
- Who does the character live with?

Personality and emotions:
- What are their main characteristics?
- What does the character think of himself/herself?
- What do others think about him/her?
- What does the character think others think about him/her?
- What does the character love?
- What does the character find funny?
- What is the character afraid of? Does the character have a secret?
- If something does not work out the way the character would want it to, or something is difficult, how does he or she react?
- What does the character want to avoid most? What does he or she do to avoid it? Or how does he or she react when it happens anyway?

Values:
- What does the character find important? Why?
- What does the character believe?
- What is the character proud of? Why?
- What does the character want to achieve? What does the character dream of? What will the character do to achieve this?

Education and job:
- Is the character at school and if so, what year are they in?
- Does the character have a job?
- Does he or she like their education or job? Why?

Relationships:
- Who are the friends of the character?
- Does the character have enemies? Who and why?
- Who does the character also see regularly?
- How do others see this character? What does he or she think of themselves?

Preferences:
- What does the character love to do in his or her free time?
- What does the character hate?
- What is the favourite food of the character?
- Favourite colours?
- Dress sense?
- Haircut?
- Looks?
- Which music does the character listen to?

Past:
Which important things happened in his/her life? (You could also make a family tree.)

Evolution:
Does the character go through an important change in the story? Which one?

APPENDIX 3

Strategic Partnership: Agents of Change (SPACE) – Pedagogical Framework

1   Introduction

The SPACE project strives for innovation by providing future teachers with the necessary know-how in order to implement interdisciplinary art/science educational approaches within the STEAM framework in European schools.

Write a Science Opera (WASO) is an interdisciplinary educational environment in which pupils explore science and art simultaneously (Ben-Horin et al., 2017). WASO activities have been implemented in many countries. The vast majority of WASO activities have been based on scientific themes in the fields of biology, physics, astronomy, and chemistry. The SPACE project aims to extend the disciplinary field to include inspiration from European space research and technology as foundations for STEAM activities. An underlying question for the current document is therefore "in what ways are STEAM activities which are inspired by innovative space-related technology and engineering different than STEAM activities inspired by other scientific themes?"

Innovation may be thought of as creativity applied (Robinson, 2011). An important issue for the SPACE project's Pedagogical Framework is, therefore, that of how the project conceptualises creativity on the road to innovation of the kind described above. This Pedagogical Framework is thereby structured in two distinct section: the first section covers the theoretical approach, and the second features a practical example of WASO implementation based on a recent European Space Agency technological development.

2   Theoretical Approach[1]

The question of how to theorise creativity within the SPACE project requires attention. We need to understand the phenomenon of creativity in the context of teaching and education and, more precisely, what it is we are doing that enables creativity to emerge. To this end, we rely on Living Dialogic Space, a theoretical approach to creativity in education, as a way of understanding creativity within the SPACE project's context and as a point of departure for a discussion about the actual, 'astronomical' role of space in the SPACE project's pedagogical frame (Chappell & Craft, 2011).

Chappell and Craft (2011) theorised Living Dialogic Space (hereafter LDS) as research spaces which enable debate and difference of opinions amongst various stakeholders in educational settings. These may be pupils, (pre-service) teachers, artists, researchers, or external persons (e.g. policy-makers). LDS enables a bottom-up approach to the educational setting, thus typically departing from "usual hierarchical, top-down power conversations expected within schools" (Craft, Chappell, & Slade, 2014, p. 364). This opens (metaphorical) spaces which promote a sense of equality among all those involved. Chappell and Craft (2011) specified LDS as an attempt to encourage risk-taking in the space between two opposing views of the educational setting: The educator's wish to implement creative teaching on the one hand, and macro-level tendencies (such as a focus on standardised testing) on the other. In order to move towards educators' implementation of creative teaching, they provided a methodological tool which exemplifies LDS and facilitates its production: the Creative Learning Conversation.

In conceptualising LDS, Chappell and Craft (1979) relied on three distinct theoretical sources: Bronfenbrenner's bio-ecological theory, Lefebvre's spatialisation of thinking, and Bakhtin's work on the subject of dialogue.

Chappell and Craft (2011) situated LDS within Bronfenbrenner's bio-ecological theory, in which local phenomena are nested in a larger ecological environment, such as the social and cultural ones. The personal level of interaction amongst individuals reflects Bronfenbrenner's concept of the microsystem. The mesosystem is comprised of multiple microsystems developing interrelationships, which in LDS can be exemplified by classroom culture or school policies. The exosystem refers to contexts which do not necessarily involve the individuals in question directly yet which affect micro and mesosystems. The exosystem may be exemplified by local educational authorities' attitudes towards creativity. The macrosystem represents the wider, more complex network of interconnected systems, which relate to ideology or governmental policy which impact school organisation or curriculum. In the context of the SPACE project, the macro-level may be exemplified by the previously-mentioned focus on performativity which has the impact of educators' often avoiding risk-taking in the lower levels of Bronfenbrenner's ecological model. Originating in the field of psychology, Bronfenbrenner critiqued psychological analysis of individuals' development which failed to take into account the impact of various levels of the ecological system on that development (Bronfenbrenner, 1979). Chappell and Craft correspondingly constructed LDS theory as a micro and mesosystem interaction with larger systems' impacts upon them as well as the individual's creativity's potential impact on her exo and macrosystems.

In their evoking of the term "space", Chappell and Craft (2011) based their theory on an understanding of the nature of spaces for which they relied on Lefebvre's work on spatialisation of thinking. Lefebvre differentiated between perceived, conceived, and lived space as parts of the social space. (He referred to physical space as "absolute space", a notion which will be returned to in the pages below.) In this view, perceived space relates to spatial practice of everyday routine. Conceived space relates to abstractions of principles such as "conceived roles and relationships" (Chappell & Craft, 2011, p. 376). Lived space relates to bodily experience. In the absence of lived space, "the imagination could never capture the experiential complexity, fullness and perhaps unknowable mystery of actual lived space" (Chappell & Craft, 2011, p. 377). Lived space is "qualitative, fluid, and dynamic" (Lefebvre, 1991, as cited in Chappell & Craft, 2011, p. 377). Within the context of the Write a Science Opera (WASO) intervention it is apparent in, for example, the extensive group work during which movement-based workshops are implemented in order to enact the drama, music, and scenography inspired by, and communicating, scientific phenomena. Lived spaces are characterised by lack of closure, and thus capacity for change realised through dialogue. Chappell and Craft rely on Bakhtin in order to theorise their use of the concept of that dialogue. Working in literary analysis, Bakhtin argued that open-ended dialogue was the "single adequate form for verbally expressing authentic life", and that "every thought and every life merges in the open-ended dialogue" (Bakhtin, 1984, as cited in Chappell & Craft, 2011, p. 377). Chappell and Craft relied on Bakhtin's work on dialogue as "shared enquiry ... forming a continuous chain of questions and answers" (Wegerif, 2010, p. 25). Bakhtin's specification of dialogue as an end in itself which enables individuals to discover both themselves and others (as co-creators) is therefore of paramount relevance (Bakhtin, 1984, p. 252). Indeed, dialogue invokes the ability to listen to others and rethink, by "identifying with the space of dialogue" (Chappell & Craft, 2011, p. 377). It is therefore precisely here that the works of Lefebvre on spatialisation and Bakhtin on dialogue meet to provide a theoretical overlap which informs LDS within the Bronfenbrenner bio-ecological system.

2.1   *Creative Learning Conversations*

In order to exemplify and create Living Dialogic Space, Chappell and Craft proposed Creative Learning Conversations as methodological devices. Creative Learning Conversations may include (but are not limited to) partnerships between teachers and artists, or co-creation of role play and games with symbolic elements which elicit discussion in educational settings (Craft et al., 2014). They allow educators and pupils to become collaborating researchers who, together, develop multiple perspectives in an environment which encourages partiality, emancipation, participation, debate, openness to action, subjectivity, and embodied and verbalised exchanges of ideas (Chappell, Craft, Rolfe, & Jobbins, 2012). In practice, Conversations involve two action types: re-positioning and listening-actioning. The former entails a change in relationships, such as when pupils and teachers interact in a flat-hierarchy environment induced by physical or metaphorical repositioning. Listening-actioning follows: Chappell and Craft (2011) observed teachers taking time to engage with pupils towards action and seriously considering pupils' ideas as a result of the methodological Conversations. Within this context, engaging with difference of roles and relations leads to change of practice, and, thereafter, changes in how pupils create. Living Dialogic Space (LDS) consequently builds upon a didactic orientation towards educational design as a common space for various stakeholders. In LDS, imagination is employed in order to, for example, allow pupils to take on roles of other stakeholders so as to enable freer debate. It is here where the Conversations enable creativity to emerge, and where LDS provides an understanding of that creativity.

As previously mentioned, another important context of Living Dialogic Space is its existence in tension with macro-level tendencies (Chappell & Craft, 2011). These largely relate to governments' striving for standardised pupil achievements which often cause creative interventions to be viewed as unjustifiable. This tension is not unique to the specific theory of Living Dialogic Space, but is rather a general reality emerging on the macro-level (Biesta, 2014). What is unique to LDS in this context, though, is Chappell and Craft's theorising LDS as a way of creating a space so as to enable educators to welcome risk-taking. And it is here where the SPACE project lays its claim to innovation by providing opportunities and necessary tools for future educators to handle that risk. Creative Learning Conversations are thus methodological devices which stimulate change by supporting partiality and subjectivity, and can both exemplify and produce Living Dialogic Space.

The SPACE project's actions must now be discussed with regard to their qualifying as creative according to the theory presented. The Write a Science Opera (WASO) intervention exemplifies the SPACE project's STEAM (Science, Technology, Engineering, Arts, Math) approach. WASO departs from a more traditional lecture-style teaching. The intervention entails art and science educators guiding and supporting pupils' creation of an original science-inspired artistic performance. Pupils explore the chosen topic by engaging with drama, music, and visual arts practices, corresponding to Creative Learning

Conversations' typical reliance on a variety of media. Activities in both science and art are constructed as physical and social occupation of shared space, enabling what Chappell and Craft (2011) termed "Living Space". The intervention necessitates an altered physical space (activities are usually realised in workshop-format and group work is the norm). A bottom-up, participatory approach is employed to generate ideas. During the intervention (which may vary in duration, extending from one day to one year), pupils establish an "opera company", and assume roles such as composers, scenographers, orchestra musicians, actors, singers, company leaders, and science or math researchers. This metaphorical re-positioning is necessary in Creative Learning Conversations, and enables pupils' interaction with teachers in a flat-hierarchy environment. Furthermore, while pupils are chosen for their opera company roles by teachers, artists, and scientists, this occurs only after those educators have considered pupils' preferences and requests for respective roles. During the intervention, many products are developed, such as songs, paintings, poems, and science communication material. These are created by using one pupil's idea as raw material for other pupils' products in a continuous, cyclical process which thus involves several pupils in each product's development. This constant negotiation of multiple perspectives exemplifies the importance of LDS theory's dialogic nature, and allows pupils to recognise their own contribution in all products. Furthermore, in LDS theory, listening-actioning entails teachers taking time to engage with pupils towards action and seriously considering their inputs as a result of the Creative Learning Conversation. This type of listening-actioning is typical of the intervention in question.

Before we attempt to describe actual (astronomical) space, it is important to specify that Lefebvre's conceptual triad does not imply a conscious shifting between various categorisations of space on the part of the subject in question (e.g. primary school pupils). Rather, it provides a way of conceptualising and producing social space within a given society (e.g. classrooms). Lefebvre described spatial practice as perceived space. Here, the SPACE project's intervention impacts pupils' everyday routine, which is largely disrupted by the innovative intervention. We observe the negotiation of those changes and ensuing social interactions with the triad's two other ideas of space. Conceived space, or Representations of space, was theorised by Lefebvre as having to do with abstraction of principles such as conceived roles and relationships of teachers, artists, students, and researchers which identify what is lived and perceived with what is conceived. This is where the SPACE project's WASO intervention offers pupils the opportunities to be cast in new roles, and learn how production of new (social) space impacts their ideas of their own learning environment. The third characterisation, and from which LDS gets its name, is lived space, or representational space. It relates to bodily experience, yet that bodily experience does not actually occur in Lived Space. Rather, it is a representation of bodily experience. It has meaning through associated images and symbols. It overlays physical space, making use of its objects. It requires openness, which Chappell and Craft (2011) claim they see in Creative Learning Conversations, where potentiality is extrapolated, shaped and constructed through physical and social occupation of shared space. For the SPACE project which is part of the STEM to STEAM movement, this is a space where meaning is made. This is where art and science meet in the ideas of the child. It is also where solving the problem of such a complex task is negotiated by the child, where physical objects such as artefacts are given symbolic meaning, and where we may make symbolic use of the stage, itself a physical object, as a science learning arena.

In order to approach Lefebvre's theory of social space more deeply, we must now observe two aspects of Karl Marx's thought (Production and Dialectic) which provided main sources of inspiration for Lefebvre.

2.2 *Production*

Marx regarded the material conditions of a society's mode of production (its way of producing the means of human existence or, in Marxist terms, the union of its productive capacity and social relations of production), as fundamental in determining its organisation and development. Marxists believe they can and should reorganise society by changing its mode of production. Lefebvre shifted towards active production of social space. For him, space was a complex social construction which included the social production of meaning. His conceptual triad can thus be seen as a framework within which to understand interplay between ideas and meanings, and their actual production. LDS theory, in turn, relies on producing new social space within the classroom. The SPACE project relies on new design for interactions within the social space in the classroom. Results of these, which adhere to a renegotiation of the mode of knowledge production, are exemplified through transferring of ownership of that production to pupils by allowing it to emerge (creatively) without dictation from educational authorities, thus relying on a flat-hierarchy structure. In the WASO intervention, nobody has complete control over the knowledge produced. It can only be produced collectively according to the methodological approach employed. Furthermore, Lefebvre's argument for a different mode of spatial production than that which reigned under capitalism (he termed the latter "abstract space") also implies an avoidance of alienating people from their own work and creativity due to a misuse of social production of space. This also informs LDS theory's support of the intervention as it seeks to avoid top-down power chains by encouraging the child's exploration of her own emerging ideas.

2.3 *Dialectic*

In Marx's approach to dialectic, ideas and material are created through their interaction. LDS theory overlays the Creative Learning Conversations practical methodology with open spaces within which to negotiate stakeholders' differences of opinion and/or perspective. In the WASO intervention, as an example, physical artefacts are constructed to allow exploration of science and art simultaneously, as different points of view. It is the creative educator's task to provide pupils with tools to create artefacts which reflect those underlying interdisciplinary ideas. The living space of dialogue corresponds to what was theoretically articulated by Lefebvre: In the Creative Learning Conversations methodology, conceptual maps, for example, or collaborative games, encourage dialogues which, then, themselves raise new questions. Now, though, we must consider the ecological placing of this in order to understand how the intervention functions: where is this occurring in relation to Bronfenbrenner's ecological model? Creative Learning Conversations create Living Dialogic Spaces strongly located in the mesosystem, in which microsystems interact. Tensions are often experienced here with external impacts of the exosystem in dialogue with microsystems. They have potential for conflict and difference, without necessary resolution, and are reflective and embodied. The dialogic dimension is where the exosystem and macro-system become visible in framing the mesosystem, and thus where the space opened up by engaging with the LDS theory to begin with, may be negotiated. In the engagement between microsystems within the mesosystem, influences, constraints, and opportunities are experienced emergent from the wider exosystem (for example of funding and priorities) and macrosystem (for example governmental policy for educational engagement). Therefore, given the dynamic nature of each ecological level, the space dimension of LDS seems highly important in locating not as a fixed or hierarchical space, as Chappell and Craft specify, but as a space of counter-possibilities, where conceptual, emotional, identity and other exploration can occur. It is therefore here that an option to governmental policies of performativity, often focussing on achievement in what is referred to as core learning areas, and an extensive reliance on quantitative test scores which focus on achievement in what some consider to be a limited way, may be exercised.

In the following section, a specific example of the extension of inspirational material for WASO activities to (astronomical) space is provided, followed by a discussion of that extension's impact on creativity in the (new) social space based on the description of LDS in section one.

3 Practical Example of WASO Implementation Based on a Recent European Space Agency Technological Development

In past years, the Write a Science Opera (WASO) educational approach has been implemented based on inspiration provided by a large variety of scientific phenomena. In this section, a first step is made towards the extension of the main inspirational source for a WASO activity to a technological development conceptualised and executed by the European Space Agency (ESA).[2]

The Solar and Heliospheric Observatory (SOHO) is a project of "international collaboration between ESA and NASA to study the Sun from its deep core to the outer corona and the solar wind" (ESA & NASA, 2018). Composed of a large variety of scientific instruments, SOHO was set in motion in 1995, and positioned 1.5 million kilometres from the earth, where the gravity of the earth and sun are in balance at Lagrange Point No. 1 or L1 (1% of the distance between the earth and sun). In this way, SOHO could "remain hovering around that relative position, in a 'halo orbit', undisturbed by sunsets, while it accompanies the Earth in its orbit round the Sun" (ESA, n.d.). In its place in space, SOHO was required to stare at the sun "without letting its telescopic eyes wander by more than a few ten-thousandths of a degree" (ESA, n.d.).

Despite the brevity of the quoted text in the paragraph above, it succeeds in providing inspiration for our example. The following questions arise: 1. Which elements of the technological endeavour should provide inspiration for our art project? 2. How do we make the transfer between the disciplines?

As is befitting an inquiry process, there is no single correct solution to either of these questions.

With regards to question 1, suffice it to say that the SPACE project considers every and any detail of the technological endeavour as ripe with enough information to spark a creative arts-infused process. With regards to question 2: The fact that SOHO was placed at 1% of the distance to the sun, for example, may be artistically interpreted in many ways (e.g. through graphical depictions of that ratio in costumes or scenography, a musical composition which accentuates every hundredth beat, etc.). The challenge of avoiding the telescopic eyes' wandering may similarly be depicted through a variety of artistic expressions (a minimalistic musical or dramatic expression, an inflexible dramaturgical expression, etc.).

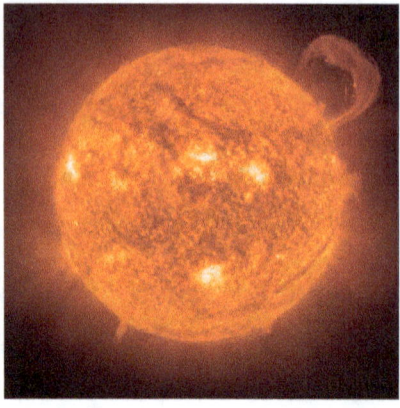

FIGURE 50
Image of a huge, handle-shaped prominence taken on September 14, 1999. Prominences are huge clouds of relatively cool dense plasma suspended in the Sun's hot, thin corona. At times, they can erupt, escaping the Sun's atmosphere.
PHOTO CREDIT: SOHO [ESA AND NASA]

Another approach to both questions 1 and 2, however, would be to find elements of the technological endeavour, or that which is discovered and/or enabled, which resonates with one or more artistic expressions. An example: One of the significant foundations providing ESA's perspective of the SOHO mission is the discovery that the sun "sings to itself".[3] While too low for human hearing, solar physicists can still detect rhythmic motions in the solar surface, produced by sound waves reverberating inside the sun. The resulting oscillations have precisely defined frequencies, like musical notes and overtones, and on analysis they give novel information about the way the sun is built.[4] And so, it is possible to begin at this end of the art/science interaction and use musical aspects of the sun to embark upon the WASO process.

Regardless of the approach chosen during each specific WASO implementation, however, it will be the creative ideas and questions of the pupils which define its character and development.

Acknowledgement

The SPACE project's Pedagogical Framework is publicly available from https://steameducation.eu/resources/Pedagogical-framework_FINAL.pdf Reprinted here with permission from the SPACE project.

Notes

1   Section 2 of the Pedagogical Framework relies on argumentations developed in the context of the Theory and Ethics of Science PhD course (VITHF900) at the University of Bergen by

PhD candidate Oded Ben-Horin (2016). The sections of material which were adapted for the purpose of Section 2 of this document were thereby used with permission.
2   While the complete description of the practical school-based implementation lies beyond the scope of this pedagogical document, the process is hereby set in motion by providing the necessary example(s) and directions for their use in the WASO process.
3   ESA, *SOHO Promotional Material.*
4   NASA, "Sounds of the Sun", https://www.nasa.gov/feature/goddard/2018/sounds-of-the-sun

References

Bakhtin, M. M. (1984). *Problems of Dostoevsky's poetics* (C. Emerson, Ed. & Trans.). Minneapolis, MN: University of Minnesota Press. Retrieved June 20, 2016, from https://monoskop.org/images/1/1d/Bakhtin_Mikhail_Problems_of_Dostoevskys_Poetics_1984.pdf

Ben-Horin, O., Chappell, K. A., Halstead, J., & Espeland, M. (2017). Designing creative inter-disciplinary science and art interventions in schools: The case of Write a Science Opera (WASO). *Cogent Education, 4*(1).

Biesta, G. J. J. (2014). *The beautiful risks of education.* Boulder, CO: Paradigm Publishers.

Bronfenbrenner, U. (1979). *The ecology of human development.* Cambridge, MA: Harvard University Press.

Chappell, K. A., & Craft, A. (2011). Creative learning conversations: Producing living dialogic spaces. *Educational Research, 53*(3), 363–385.

Chappell, K. A., Craft, A. R., & Rolfe, L. M., & Jobbins, V. (2012). Humanizing creativity: Valuing our journeys of becoming. *International Journal of Education & the Arts, 13*(8).

Craft, A., Chappell, D., & Slade, C. (2014). *D2.1 CREAT-IT pedagogical framework.* CREAT-IT. Retrieved June 19, 2018, from www.creatit-project.eu

ESA. (n.d.). *SOHO promotional material.* Paris, France: European Space Agency Public Relations Division.

ESA & NASA. (2018). *About the SOHO mission.* SOHO, Solar and Heliospheric Observatory. Retrieved from https://sohowww.nascom.nasa.gov/about/about.html

Lefebvre, H. (1991). *The production of space.* Cambridge, UK: Wiley-Blackwell.

NASA. (n.d.). *Sounds of the sun.* Retrieved from https://www.nasa.gov/feature/goddard/2018/sounds-of-the-sun

Robinson, K. (2011). *Out of our minds. Learning to be creative.* Oxford, UK: Capstone.

Wegerif, R. (2010). *Mind expanding: Teaching for thinking and creativity in primary education.* Maidenhead, UK: Open University Press.

www.ingramcontent.com/pod-product-compliance
Lightning Source LLC
Chambersburg PA
CBHW070627300426
44113CB00010B/1686